Inevitable Illusions

How Mistakes of Reason Rule Our Minds

MASSIMO PIATTELLI-PALMARINI

TRANSLATED BY
MASSIMO PIATTELLI-PALMARINI
AND KEITH BOTSFORD

John Wiley & Sons, Inc.
New York • Brisbane • Chichester • Toronto • Singapore

Copyright © 1994 by Massimo Piattelli-Palmarini
Published by John Wiley & Sons, Inc.

First published in Italy as *L'Illusione Di Sapere* and adapted
into English by Massimo Piattelli-Palmarini and Keith Botsford.

Library of Congress Cataloging-in-Publication Data:
Piattelli-Palmarini, Massimo.
    [Illusione di sapere.   English]
    Inevitable illusions : how mistakes of reason rule our minds   /
Massimo Piattelli-Palmarini ;   translated by Massimo Piattelli-
Palmarini and Keith Botsford.
       p.   cm.
    Includes bibliographical references and index.
    ISBN 0-471-58126-7 (cloth : alk. paper)
    1. Reasoning (Psychology)   2. Prejudices.   3. Illusion
(Philosophy)   4. Thought and thinking.   I. Title.
BF442.P5213 1994
153.4'3—dc20   94-12759

Printed in the United States of America

10 9 8 7 6 5 4 3 2 1

For Amos Tversky and Daniel Kahneman

Contents

Preface

In the spring of 1991 I published, in Italy, a book on education. Its instant success, consecrated by some 100,000 readers, left me dumbfounded. Even more unexpected, just as I was completing the manuscript for this new book in the winter of 1993, was the success of the French translation of the earlier book (nearly 30,000 copies sold).

Understandably, many friends were already curious about the contents of my new book, and kept asking, "Just what's this new book about?"

And I would reply, perhaps too hastily, "About our mental tunnels."

"Hmm. Sounds interesting. And what's that?" they asked. "Can you give us an example?"

After a few attempts, I finally found the perfect example, based on geography. It worked beautifully with my Italian and French friends, for reasons I shall explain in a moment, but the flavor of it can be preserved by a couple of analogous examples from the geography of the American continents.

Let's draw a vertical line straight up from Caracas, the capital of Venezuela, right along the meridian. What major city in the United States would we find on the same line? Try to guess, without looking it up in an atlas.

Now imagine that we take off in a helicopter from Los Angeles and hover over the city for a moment. Again, without checking on any chart, let's guess the "true" compass course our helicopter should hold if we want to fly to Reno, Nevada. What's your guess?

The prevailing answers are, respectively, to the first question New Orleans, or Dallas, and to the second question some 10 to 20 degrees east. The correct answers, amazing as they seem to many, are instead Boston and 20 degrees *west* (or equivalently, if you prefer, 340 degrees on the compass).

The examples based on the geography of Italy were of the same ilk, but probably more striking for a native-born Italian. As every Italian knows, the "boot" of Italy doesn't come straight down out of Europe. In fact it's at a steep angle, a sort of diagonal, like the coastline running north from New York City. So I said to my Italian and French friends, "Let's draw a straight line down from Marseille to the right. Now, what big Italian city would you run into?" Most of my friends said, "Genoa."

Now, if you were to draw a vertical line straight up from the heel of Italy, right along the meridian, what European capital would you find on the same line? Here I'll bet the average person would answer, "Vienna," or maybe, "Brussels."

One more. Take off in a helicopter from Naples in a straight line and head for Trieste. What's your flight path? Again, most people would say, "10 to 20 degrees east."

Where's the tunnel vision? If the reader has the same perplexed reaction as my friends, we're making progress; let's pause for a moment on these geographical intuitions. Ask around and check just how common these intuitions are, and how stubborn we are about them. Then pick up a map and ascertain the truth of the matter. You will quickly find out that Marseille is on the same latitude as . . . Siena, significantly to the south and east of Genoa; that from the heel of Italy going straight north you wind up in Budapest; and that Trieste is west of Naples. Yes, the boot of Italy is at a very great angle to the Continent.

Odd, isn't it? What happened to us? Is it that we don't know how to read a map? Do we lack memory? No, the curious fact is that in our heads, and without our knowing it, the boot of Italy is rotated clockwise so that it seems to lie north–south. All the replies we innocently, but with such conviction, gave to those questions derive from this incomprehensible rotation in our minds. No one forced us to do this, nor is this rotation something we learned in school. Indeed, it is not something we have learned, not in *any* sense of the word *learn*. Having repeatedly studied maps, we should have realized how things actually were, and we should have corrected this variation. But all unbeknownst to us, even furtively, our minds have played this trick on us. They play the same trick on everyone, and *each time in exactly the same way.* No one, but absolutely no one, ever "rotates" the boot of Italy in the opposite direction, and toward the horizontal.

It would be amazing if *only* we Italians were subject to this sort of geographical illusion. But in fact we are in good company. The same process makes Americans think that Reno, Nevada, is to the east of Los Angeles (when in fact it's to the west) and that Rome lies to the south of New York City (when in fact it's north of New York City, which is directly in line with Naples). Nor do most Americans realize that when they fly due south from Detroit, the first country they'll come to is . . . Canada. And so on.

This sort of geographical illusion is the simplest and most striking example of what I call "tunnel vision." This book is about many other examples, taken from the most varied fields.

At this point, I hope, you begin to suspect that there just *might* be some *systematically* and universally odd factor at work in our minds, and at work quite unconsciously. But why use so dark and threatening a term as *tunnel?* These mental and geographical quirks may amuse us, indeed make us curious, but they do not *alarm* us. The purpose of this book is to show that we ought to be alarmed, that there's a *lot* to be alarmed about. Not in these geographical oddities, but because we all have cognitive illusions of this kind and scale (that is, both gross and macroscopic). And these extend right up to our vital decision-making capacity. As we shall see, even when we are engaged in high-level administration, in the courts, in the hospital, or in the family, we are all prey to certain cognitive illusions. *And* we are deluded in complete innocence, in good faith, not even realizing that we are so misled. Quite without distinction, politicians, generals, surgeons, and economists as much as vendors of salami and ditchdiggers are all, without being aware of it, and even when they are in the best of humors and while exercising their professions, subject to a myriad of such illusions. The current term for this is "cognitive" illusions, to indicate that they exist quite apart from any subjective, emotional illusion and from any other such habitual, classical, irrational distortions. The pages that follow provide ample documentation, and contain suggestions as to how we may take urgent and sensible precautions against these illusions.

It never ceases to surprise me that, more or less 20 years after these illusions were first discovered, and after dozens of books and hundreds of articles have been printed on the subject of cognitive illusions, almost no one except for a select circle of specialists seems to have taken this discovery seriously.

Acknowledgments

I t would be impossible to express here my deep gratitude to all those individuals and institutions that have made this book possible. First and foremost, I owe an immense debt to the main researchers in this field, Amos Tversky and Daniel Kahneman, to whom this book is dedicated. They provided not only constant inspiration and a flow of new ideas, but also several stimulating conversations. Over the years, they also fed me their most recent data and interpretations, often before publication, and were kind enough to read a previous version of this manuscript, offering much-needed advice and criticism.

Special thanks are due to Eldar Shafir of Princeton University, with whom I have been lucky to interact ever since he was a graduate student at MIT and who is now one of the truly top professionals in this field. He kindly undertook the burden of reading successive versions of the manuscript, helping me weed out many imprecisions and unclarities.

In the fall of 1992, thanks to an invitation by Zenon Pylyshyn to teach a graduate course on this subject at Rutgers

University, I was able to note—thanks to my awe-inspiring "students" Jerry Fodor, Jacques Mehler, Steven Stich, and Chuck Schmidt—the difficulties inherent in measuring the impact of cognitive illusions on a full-blown theory of rationality.

The first-rate intellectual and human climate of the Massachusetts Institute of Technology, where I've had the opportunity to build my research and teaching for the past nine years, contributed significantly to my work in this field. Among my present and past MIT colleagues, I owe a special debt to Daniel N. Osherson and James T. Higginbotham.

A variety of illuminating hints and suggestions also came from Ned Block, George Boolos, Susan Carey, Joshua Cohen, Paul Horwich, and Robert Stalnaker. Alan Hein, Steven Pinker, and Emilio Bizzi have been particularly supportive of my undergraduate class "Rationality and Cognition" at MIT, and several of the brightest students helped me refine ideas and ways of conveying them, in particular Nick Cassimatis, who is the kind of student every teacher dreams of teaching.

Although Eric Wanner, then the director of the Alfred P. Sloan Foundation, initially brought me to MIT with a different plan in mind, an unexpected turn of events brought us a shared, active interest in cognitive illusions. Eric is now, as president of the Russel Sage Foundation, giving an unprecedented boost to this whole field and has wisely gathered the best of the best for prolonged periods every year to focus on the hardest of the hard.

Mitch Kapor generously helped both the MIT Center for Cognitive Science and my own research, continuing to make it all possible.

I am especially indebted to Keith Botsford, not only for his outstanding translation and painstaking editing of this manuscript, but also for having started the writing process in the first place by encouraging me to publish an article in his prestigious magazine *Bostonia* in April 1991. The resulting success of that piece surprised us both. Already twice reprinted in psychology textbooks and used by teachers in several U.S. universities, that article, and Keith's generous support, were the seeds from which this book grew.

The process of turning the seed into a tree has been admirably accomplished by Emily Loose of John Wiley & Sons in the English-speaking world; by Gian Arturo Ferrari and Marco Vigevani of Mondadori in Italy; and by Odile Jacob, of Editions Odile Jacob, in France. I thank them all.

Finally, a brief prophecy and a challenge: I am persuaded that, sooner or later, Amos Tversky and Daniel Kahneman will win the Nobel Prize for economics. When on some October day this news reaches the daily papers, readers of this book will be able to say, with a certain self-satisfaction, as their friends and colleagues try to decipher those complicated names: "Sure, Tversky and Kahneman. You mean you don't know? They are the ones who . . . ."

January 1994
Marblehead, Massachusetts

Introduction

I n simple and basic fashion, this book proposes to set out the recent scientific discovery of *an* unconscious. Not the unconscious or subconscious explored by psychoanalysis, but one that *always and unbeknownst to us* involves the cognitive: that is, the world of reason, of judgment, of the choices to be made among different opportunities, of the difference between what we consider probable and what we consider unlikely. The fundamental materials of psychoanalysis are brought to light by studying dreams, what we repress, our notorious complexes, our *lapsus linguae*, the ways we convert imagined symptoms into real illnesses (our somata), our wish fulfillments, and many ill-concealed incongruities in our feelings. In contrast, the material we deal with in this book derives from the texts of economics, from the stock exchange, from the boardrooms of business, from clinical consultation, from the mechanism by which public opinion is manipulated, and from electoral fluctuations—in fact, from wherever we make decisions "under uncertainty." In short, our examples are based on phenomena found almost anywhere, in almost anyone, and just about at any moment.

As Freud did in his work, we deal here with an individual, not a collective subconscious, with psychological mechanisms that affect single individuals without their realizing it. These often have tangible and undesirable, if not catastrophic, effects on society. This cognitive unconscious is a trait that, despite differences of culture, in talent or fashion, *each and every one of us* must be ready to recognize when taking stock of the somewhat disorganized inventory of human nature. Almost certainly we inherit these illusions, their knotlike intersections, and our tunnel vision from the evolution of our species. They may well have been of the greatest possible utility at some remote time. They may have saved our ancient ancestors from wild beasts and famine, but even granted that such a simpleminded Darwinism should have actually been at work in their creation, for a very long time these illusions have been no more than a burden. Darwinism or not, we should all learn how to protect ourselves, individually and collectively, from the effects of our cognitive subconscious.

As one might expect when we are alerted to a discovery of this kind, we quickly learn to read the signs that reveal this sort of mental mechanism, which are all around us and within us. The same thing happened with Freud from the moment when his discoveries became part of our general mental baggage. In a way, then, this book leads to a new form of mental hygiene, and gives us a way to develop it.

Though it is very much a part of today's culture, the idea that our reason should take over an everextending field, saving us from the excessive disorder of our "spontaneity," is still being received with some concern. In this field we have to be ready to understand and overcome a number of psychological resistances. By what psychoanalyst friends tell me, in the field of the emotional subconscious, the emotional resistances to be overcome are no longer the ones most people felt in Freud's, that is, our grandparents', day. The moralizing respectability and the fear of sex evidenced in Freud's day no longer exist. I am told that today's resistances come in the form of summary, seemingly pitiless and unrelenting "wild" self-analyses offered up by those who claim to have understood "everything" about themselves. We no longer just reject the true, slow, and difficult self-analysis, we do so by an excess of disordered, instant auto-diagnoses that seem both sincere and cruel. I expect some similar reaction in those who read these pages.

The main resistance to rationality in this new field of cognitive studies is our insistence on the correctness of our intuitive strategies, our pseudo-reasoning; we exercise considerable ingenuity in demonstrating that these are not so "disorderly as they seem." I anticipate that a frequent response by someone caught *in flagrante delicto* in one of our model problems will be to find a counter-example, a case that is *different* from that onto which we have stumbled, but one for which our "wild" intuition might give a *vaguely* plausible account. Having established this insecure and irrelevant point of departure, our cognitive subconscious finds it easy to pass to the "demonstration" that "therefore" all is well. Between rationality and our cognitive pride, we will choose the latter, and are willing to pay whatever the price for so doing. In short, we are more disturbed to have to admit, in 1994, that we are *instinctively* very poor evaluators of probability and equally poor at choosing between alternative possibilities, than to admit that in some recondite depth of our instincts we have symbolically desired one parent and sought to kill the other.

Freud made a lapidary observation: that where there is now the subconscious, one day the "I" will surface. Thanks to one of those jewels that are hidden deep in language, his original phrase *also* could be read as saying, "Where that was, I should be: *Wo Es war, soll Ich werden.*" His maxim meant that reclaiming rationality eventually *must* account for entanglements in general and entanglements that we have within ourselves but of which we are not *intuitively* aware. With a very different method, different presuppositions, and different material, this book undertakes a project like Freud's, with the aim of expanding reason. It is important to underline, in

Freud's dictum, the word *ought* (*sollen*). For this project, like Freud's, also has a *moral* dimension: to restore our decisional health.

My hope is that readers will be astounded, even thrown off balance, by discovering, through concrete examples, this cognitive subconscious in themselves. The idea is to motivate the reader to learn to resist the powerful temptation within all of us to enter, and even to pursue to the end, the tunnels I will describe. What these are, and why I call them that, I'll come to in a moment. But the ultimate aim of this book is to go beyond our initial stupefaction, to consider many subjects in our public and private lives under a new light, and thus raise many of our spontaneous judgments to a different, higher, and more rational plane.

The problem of rationality is a perennial one, though every age deals with it in a different way. Aristotle sought to discover the internal laws of reason; he wanted to make them intelligible, explicitly transmissible, and hence susceptible to being taught. The Enlightenment sought to demonstrate that reason is both necessary and *sufficient* to the ordering of human affairs. The romanticists and relativists (of both yesterday and today), believing they could exist beyond reason, were compelled to denounce its limitations. Modern rationalists, from Kant onward, have tried to explore its internal boundaries, arguing that it is neither possible nor thinkable to go outside reason (as though reason were a distant planet) to observe it.

Our own times have inherited a dilemma: Is reason a natural component or datum of our species, or is it a painfully arrived at objective that does violence to *some* of our natural tendencies? The dilemma is hardly new, but a new direction, one that looks to solutions that were unthinkable just a short time ago, was taken some 15 years ago with the systematic, dispassionate study of *how* we reason in certain model cases. This revolution in the theory of rationality, even though it is little talked about beyond a few hundred specialists in many different countries, is in full development.

The frontiers (one has to use the plural) between what is and what isn't rational are sometimes very difficult to draw. There are also, as we will see in a moment (with the perplexing results of the French pool on happiness and health), many zones of gray. Several different *kinds* of strategies are used in our intuitive reasoning. Some are suitably close to the good norms of rationality, whereas others depart sharply from them. The main lesson to be drawn from experimental research in this domain is that these strategies *coexist* in our mind, thus justifying, at least to a certain degree, *both* the sweeping claim that we are naturally rational *and* the opposite sweeping claim that we are naturally irrational. It would be legitimate, but pointless, to conclude that the truth lies somewhere in between. The results of ongoing scientific research, as the following pages testify, are much more subtle and interesting. Depending on the exact formulation of the task at hand, specific reasoning strategies are reproducibly elicited in our mind, and even slightly different formulations can sometimes produce a switch, shifting the delicate balance between coexisting intuitions and strategies, between spontaneous rationality and spontaneous irrationality. The problem is not one of "defining," or "re-defining," the notion of rationality itself, but rather one of charting the mental routes that naturally lead to certain intuitive beliefs, judgments, and preferences, and then assessing the relative merits and shortcomings of the ensuing decisions. The ultimate measuring instruments are those offered by pure logic, probability theory, economics, and decision theory. These disciplines are also, like cognitive science, in a healthy state of continuous flux, yet they usually offer criteria that are firm enough to convert our spontaneous intuitions into "hard currency." What is rational and what is irrational, *given the specific problem that we are trying to solve,* can often be decided not in terms of sheer "taste," but in terms of dollars that would have been gained (or lost) by us, with a precisely specified probability, had our decisions been guided by a certain line of reasoning. The idea of converting the lofty notion of rationality into hard currency may sound too prosaic, at least to noneconomists, but many standard problems offering precise choices between lotteries are of great help also in assessing the rationality of our probabilistic intuitions in non-monetary matters. Moreover, the scientific study of reasoning is a forbidding task, and one of the most fruitful approaches to a complicated problem is to disassemble it into pieces, study each piece separately, and then reassemble as many pieces as possible back into the larger structure. One way of proceeding, therefore, is to create interesting situations in which decisions are elicited about bets and then count the odds and the dollars (or, at any rate, measure some amount of quantifiable "utilities") associated with the various decisions. Ever since the "doctrine of chances" turned into a science, about three centuries ago, this procedure has helped in gaining a substantially better understanding of what is a rational choice, and why. We will see how delicate, but also how compelling, it is to generalize from decisions about monetary gambles to other kinds of decisions under uncertainty.

Experimental science has, as a result, taken the place of pure philosophy, constructing models concrete enough to be reproducible, meaningful, and controllable but at the same time general enough to reveal certain *fundamental* mental mechanisms that we set into motion in our daily lives. Especially interesting have been reasoning tests which should have been soluble by using specific, abstract rules of the kind well classified by psychologists, logicians, economists, and decision theorists, but that instead are solved by most of us in a rather different and impromptu way. It has been discovered that we often use a somewhat anomalous form of intuition, and adopt—often unknowingly—a number of little rules not just different from but also *incompatible* with the golden rules of rationality. It seems that all of us employ, and pursue to their end, some genuine and easy (as well as fallacious) shortcuts in our minds. Finding a shortcut is usually a good thing, but in these cases the shortcuts serve to render our thinking inaccessible to correction; they lead us to a quite different destination from that at which we intended to arrive. What is worse is that we don't even realize we have arrived "somewhere else." In good faith, we think we have really arrived at our destination and solved the problem put to us. We reason in an intuitive, impromptu fashion, and are often convinced that we have really reasoned. Hence we insist on the accuracy of our intuitions and conclusions. These are cases in which we truly don't listen to reason.

The image of one who uses such shortcuts (which in our jargon we call "heuristics") or one of those "tunnels" (which we call "biases") and follows it through is *not* that of the man who is perplexed by a problem he faces, or that of the man whose mental eye has explored a number of solutions and, not knowing how to decide which is best, simply picks one at random. As we shall see, we instead feel like someone who knows exactly how to respond. We feel that our shortcuts, on which we base our replies, are so correct as to be incontestable. The best and most striking instance of this, the super blind spot known as the "three boxes," appears at the end of this book. But there are many other cases, some of them much simpler, in which we completely fail to realize how irrational are our choices and judgments. Our response, which we know full well to be like that of a majority of the public, seems so obvious, so "natural," so "correct," that we can't even intuit that we *could* be wrong.

In France, some 20 years ago, a detailed and methodical survey was conducted as to the *subjective* factors that contributed to happiness. To much praise, the opinion poll was conducted with a statistical model based on a large and well-balanced sample of the entire population, and by an officially approved institution. The results were then published, in summary form, in the mass circulation *Le Nouvel Observateur.* There were many things, besides the unusual and intelligent nature of this survey, that I found striking, such as that money came well down the list and that the most important factor turned out to be "another person." Next to that came "the full realization of one's own potential." In the very last place came "to be in good health." The same survey included a series of questions about factors causing unhappiness. Curiously enough, a single factor—that of *not* being in good health—came first as a factor in *un*happiness. This seems perfectly normal to us and in certain model situations it can even be rationally justified, yet it is instructive to ponder awhile on this very rudimentary case, extracted from real life, of what the experts call "the intransitivity of preferences."

The "obvious" explanation for this result was underlined in the French magazine: being in good health is something we *presuppose* when we ask ourselves what makes us happy. But when we are asked to list what might contribute to our unhappiness, ill health "obviously" comes first on the list. And that's right, isn't it? Many psychologists have confirmed, by way of carefully administered tests, that something we consider "normal" does not count as a possible "cause" of an "abnormal" outcome. If we are asked to explain why Jones missed his daily commuter train yesterday, we will inquire about the *un*usual things he did, or the unusual things that happened to him, not about anything he does every day. If I mention in the story about Jones (as psychologists have done in well-controlled experiments) that he stopped in a bar to have a drink, *that* will be picked up as the cause of his subsequent mishap. Let's ask anyone to freely alter the story in such a way that Jones, contrary to fact, would have been able to get on his train, and the drink at the bar will be the item most naturally deleted from the story. Any other unusual item we may want to alternatively introduce into the story about Jones (a broken shoelace, a chance encounter with a relative from out of town) will be "naturally" singled out as "the" cause.

Thus, being in good health is considered normal, and therefore not an eligible cause of the "abnormal" state of happiness, while being in poor health (considered abnormal) can well be a signal causal factor of unhappiness (also seen as abnormal).

"What's so interesting about the results of this French poll?" the reader asks. What is interesting is that we are on our way to discovering in ourselves a mild instance of the infamous "intransitivity of preferences."

Let's imagine that Mr. Baker says he prefers strawberries to ice cream and ice cream to rice pudding. Suppose he then stoutly declares that he far prefers rice pudding to strawberries. Most of us, I think, would shake our heads and think that when it came to desserts, Mr. Baker was a little crazy. In this exceedingly crude imaginary case, we could easily capitalize on Mr. Baker's erratic and irrational tastes to fill our pockets. For no outlay whatever, and without being in a position to offer any sort of dessert, we offer Baker, at a price Baker can set himself, any one of these three desserts.

Say Baker chooses strawberries. There is agreement. But now, for just five cents more, we offer him another dessert, the one he says he prefers to strawberries: rice pudding. And if a nickel is too much to pay, we are willing to take a penny, or a mill—if such a coin still existed. Surely Baker's preference for rice pudding over strawberries is worth at least a penny? Given the fact that Baker's irrational preferences are a closed circle (he reverts to strawberries after having chosen ice cream and rice pudding, and so on), the scam can go on forever. At a penny a choice, we are still going to make money.

There's a little lesson in here: Mr. Baker's preferences are irrational because they are "intransitive." It is a bit like believing that Calcutta is larger than New York City, and that New York City is larger than Boston, but not believing that Calcutta is larger than Boston. The property "being larger than" does not "carry on" to the next item, which means it is not "transitive." In the domain of preferences (and in the domain of bets based on beliefs we firmly entertain), he who does not "carry on" from one to the next (harboring in his mind a set of preferences that is not "transitively" ordered) becomes a sort of money pump for a shrewd and unscrupulous bookmaker. As we will see, decision theory and the calculation of probabilities prove what our intuition has already, thanks to Mr. Baker, informed us: that to have even a single "glitch" in our preferences (such as intransitivity) logically implies that we may indeed become a source of funds for whoever knows how to take advantage of the fact. The awful part of this is that, given our sincere and incorrigible set of preferences and that single glitch, we fall into the trap with our own consent.

The case of the three desserts is so simpleminded that we are quickly aware of its peculiarity. But in the case of our opinion about happiness and health, as expressed in the poll, our choice seems perfectly "normal." Indeed, the two cases are somewhat alike, as are the consequences to which they may lead. A shrewd insurance agent might "innocently" propose a special policy. For the modest sum of 10 dollars he guarantees us good health for the rest of our natural lives.

Well, how can we refuse? Here are my 10 dollars. Off they go into his trouser pocket. *Now* he knows that we feel sure about our health, so, remembering our response to the questionnaire about happiness, we no longer worry about our health. Now he offers to swap that policy against another. This one guarantees us the full realization of our potential, or the boundless love of "another" of our choice. The price? Another 10 dollars. Again, how can we refuse? Given our preferences as expressed in the poll, the sum seems modest enough, and we'll certainly swallow the bait.

But no sooner have we done so that we realize with horror, the ink barely dry on the policy, that we are no longer guaranteed good health. What do we do? We panic. But our Faustian insurance salesman has yet another policy up his sleeve. This one—for the modest sum of 10 dollars—simply reverts to the first policy and once again guarantees our good health. Again, how can we refuse? This is money well spent. But in fact we are 30 bucks poorer—and *ready to start the whole cycle again,* for an infinite number of times.

This scenario is admittedly more than a bit contrived and would not pass more severe tests, but it has the advantage of being simple and very intuitive, and pointing us to the fact that the results of the French poll were not, after all, *so* obvious and natural. Simplifying it further, it surely stands to reason that cruel torture would be a strong cause of extreme unhappiness, whereas the absence of it would count as a poor candidate for being a cause of happiness. Simple numerical cases can be offered in which the results of the poll come out as *literally* rational. One would not want to turn the results of the French poll into a knock-down instance of patent irrationality, yet there is merit to the suggestion that being guaranteed good health should come first on both scales (the one that lists the factors that cause happiness and the one that lists those factors that, if missing, cause unhappiness). Otherwise, we may be easily induced to buy the series of insurance policies from the astute swindler, and lose money in an unstoppable cyclical fashion. As the survey set out to show, the replies may well be "natural," but they are not entirely "correct" in the sense that they are not entirely defensible from a rational point of view. The person who has the great misfortune to be in ill health knows perfectly well how irrational is that spontaneous, unthinking attitude of those who are healthy toward the "purely hypothetical" possibility of illness.

An old proverb says that we all spend the first half of our lives ruining our health and the second half looking after it. To take one's health for granted, to pay no heed to it while seeking a thousand other benefits—often at the cost of that good health—causes us, the moment we note the first symptoms of a serious illness, instant and bitter repentance. Theoretically, we all know this, but in one way or another we have "forgotten" about it. This is a mild proof of some irrationality in our dealing with the issues of happiness and health.

A slightly more elaborate situation, involving beliefs about probabilities and bets based on those beliefs, would be one that evokes the much feared "Dutch bookie." The diabolical Dutch bookmaker (who is not Dutch at all but universal, and makes book on everything not just horse races) no sooner discovers a glitch in our probabilistic beliefs than he offers us a series of bets such that we will lose money *come what may*. These bets do indeed *appear* to us, both singly and wholesale, as perfectly "fair," yet condemn us to become money pumps for the Dutch bookie. The interesting lesson from cases of Dutch bookies is that we are not condemned by the bookie, who only exploits our innermost tendencies, nor by our betting behaviors there and then, but rather by the deep-seated set of beliefs that ultimately motivate those bets. Probability calculus and decision theory demonstrate that there is no *rational* and persuasive method to preserve the intuitions that make us willingly accept those bets *and* stop us from becoming buyers-cum-money-pumps for the Dutch bookie. Let's examine a simple example, one that is standard in teaching probability theory and that has been polished to perfection by Daniel N. Osherson in a forthcoming volume, aptly entitled, *Invitation to Cognitive Science.* Try it, and you will see for yourself what it means to be in the grip of a Dutch bookie.

The Three-Card Problem

There are three cards in a hat. One is red on both sides (the red-red card), one is white on both sides (the white-white card), one is red on one side and white on the other (the red-white card). A single card is drawn randomly and tossed into the air.

Let's think carefully about the following three simple questions:

1. What is the probability that the red-red card was drawn?
2. What is the probability that the drawn card lands with a white side up?
3. What is the probability that the red-red card was drawn, *assuming that the drawn card lands with a red side up?*

What is your answer to each question? Would you accept a wager (small denominations) on the basis of your answers? I assume you would. Now consider the following two questions, which are a sort of contrary to the previous (2) and (3):

2'. What is the probability that the drawn card lands with a red side up?

3′. What is the probability that the red-red card was *not* drawn, assuming that the drawn card lands with a red side up?

A final touch, and a typically Dutch one at that:

4. What is the probability that the drawn card lands with a red side up, assuming that *the red-red card was drawn*?

It is safe to guess that our answer to the last question is "100 percent." Isn't it? It is also safe to say, on the basis of many experiments carried out on this case with many subjects, that we are in the grip of the Dutch bookie. In other words, if we are disposed to accept wagers on the basis of our well-pondered answers to *all* of these questions (as we should), then we are going to lose money *come what may*. Our probabilistic intuitions have already thrown us into a bottomless pit. (In what follows, we will see many more examples.) The explanation of this case is intriguing and very instructive (see "Tunnel Exits"), but the lesson is clear already. We cannot *both* maintain our intuitions *and* avoid a *sure* loss of hard money. Those intuitions of ours are demonstrably irrational. Yet they are shared by all of us, and sound very, very compelling. Upon better reasoning, and some effort, we will *have* to correct them. It would be *irrational* to maintain them, in the light of a full explanation of this case. This is a paradigm case of what we encounter in the following pages: A certain intuition, or a set of related intuitions, is shared by us all, and is perceived as very convincing, yet it has to be thrown overboard. Why? An easy and blunt way of putting it is, "Because rationality requires that it be so."

The "silly" example of Mr. Baker and the real-life (though fragile) example of the French poll were just introductions to hard-line cases such as this one. In the three-card problem there is a full-blown mathematical explanation for what is wrong in our spontaneous intuitions. The Dutch book into which we have been lured serves as a precise diagnosis of one *type* of irrationality to which all of us are subject. Very precisely, it shows that deep within ourselves we have some *anomalous* systems of mental representations that lead us, for instance, to beliefs about probabilities and fair wagers. When we act according to those beliefs, as it is perfectly natural for us to do, we *inevitably* become the prey of situations in which we lose under *every* conceivable state of affairs. Yet, the mere fact that we intuitively come to see the situation as anomalous is not sufficient to set us right. It requires thought, and thought based on real data (such as those offered by the cases in this book) *and* on well-constructed theories that can ultimately and persuasively gain our assent. That is how rationality is fostered.

To talk of the intransitivity of preferences and of Dutch bookmakers and how it is that we can will ourselves to become money pumps may seem abstruse and boring. The very fact that we turn our backs on such abstract concepts is, however, an unpardonable resistance to the progress of reason. The game is worth it, because these are important matters for all of us; they are fundamental to ourselves and to those whom we love. It is never too late to take them into account.

In the pages that follow, I describe other situations and show other mental deformations that are equally "natural" to all of us. I try hard not to be abstruse, and I even hope to be entertaining. A little effort on the part of the reader is, however, required: We will *begin* to improve ourselves precisely when we can deal with these very abstractions.

Perhaps turning gastronomy upside down, but not the logic of discovering our cognitive unconscious, I began with the three desserts. Mr. Baker and the French poll seemed an effective way to begin. These examples should not bring a bemused smile to our lips. We have, after all, just seen how we can all be, and in matters far more serious than choosing a dessert, Mr. Bakers.

Unfortunately, the incoherence of our choices, both individual and collective, extends to many fields and has disastrous social, economic, and political results. Even if we eliminated dishonesty and unbridled egotism, these tunnels of the mind would still be with us. These are errors, as we shall see, made in good faith; they can only be rectified by becoming conscious of the elementary mechanisms, many of them innate, of our thought. For the cognitive illusions with which we have to deal are totally independent of motives or emotional factors. They are hard to correct spontaneously, but they can, with a little steady work, be put right by anyone who becomes aware of them. Those irrationalities of ours are multiple; they are insidious, subterranean, and exceedingly *specific.* We review the main ones and give them their proper names, one by one.

If, in spite of all, the results of that survey on happiness continue to seem obvious to us; if my argument about the Faustian insurance salesman still strikes you as weak; if we still find it "logical" not to consider our health when we think of happiness, and think of our missing health only when considering unhappiness, then the influence of this cognitive unconscious is manifestly at work in us and should be clear. Just as clear should be the ways in which we resist uncovering that unconscious. The time has come to draw back the curtain.

CHAPTER 1

Cognitive Illusions

St. Louis, Missouri, can be proud of possessing the largest optical illusion ever created by the hand of man. The celebrated arch, which soars over the city's downtown, is exactly as wide as it is high. The reader can satisfy herself that this is true simply by using a ruler to measure the dimensions of Figure 1.

What is highly interesting is not just the surprise we feel when we verify the truth of this fact, but also the *persistence* of the optical illusion. Even after we have measured the arch, it continues to appear far taller than it is wide. Optical illusions are indeed created in just that fashion: *The eye sees what it sees, even when we know what we know.* The purpose of this book is to demonstrate that phenomena identical to optical illusions exist in the world of thought. All unbeknownst to us, there are many phenomena—all of them well studied by cognitive scientists, especially in the past 15 years—that show that some parts of our minds are unable to use knowledge available to us in other parts of our minds. As with the eye, our mental "modules" remain impervious to the corrections offered by logic,

FIGURE 1

Source: The New York Public Library

arithmetic, and rational judgment and, as we shall see, above all by our calculations as to probability.

We are therefore all of us easy prey to various "cognitive illusions": that is, to the illusion of "knowing." These are errors we commit without knowing that we do so, in good faith and errors that we often defend with vehemence, thus making our power of reasoning subservient to our illusions. Cognitive illusions, in the words of researchers Amos Tversky and Daniel Kahneman, are "neither rational nor capricious." There is nothing rational in continuing to see the St. Louis arch as higher than it is wide, even when we *know* this is not so. But no one sees it as broader than it is high. The illusion, therefore, is as they say neither rational nor capricious. All those who look at the arch are drawn in the same direction. It makes us fall into the same perceptual "tunnel."

Exactly the same thing happens with cognitive illusions. There are tunnels that, thanks to our mental processes, we unwittingly enter with heads lowered. That these tunnels exist, and that they have a dramatic effect, we shall shortly see. The discovery is recent, but the phenomenon itself is as old as our species; these tunnels are part of our human baggage.

Two concepts are fundamental here: the heuristic and the "tunnel effect," best summed up in the word *bias. Heuristic* is a somewhat off-putting and intimidating word. It derives from the same Greek root as eureka, having to do with something found or discovered. Heuristics are specific mental strategies used to solve specific problems. A heuristic might be said to be something that we "do," whereas a bias is something that "happens" to us. The so-called cognitive revolution, however, has taught us to subvert the fundamentals of these traditional concepts. For instance, in the St. Louis arch, the heuristic that we unknowingly put into play—what our eye "does"—is *automatically* to heighten a shape that soars skyward and thins rapidly as it rises, just as the actual arch does. The eye does something, and something also happens to us, which is not really something that *we* do. The examples that follow demonstrate how many things "happen" to us, even in the world of intuitions and of things we take in at a glance.

To continue with this analysis—the differences between what we do, what happens to us, and what is innate within us—we can say that a tunnel of the mind, a bias, is something we have within us. To enter one of these tunnels head down, blindly, without even knowing we are doing so, is something that happens to us. Continuing to use these distinctions, we can say that a heuristic is the specific and potent inner impulse that allows us to stray into a certain tunnel or bias. These are metaphors, and should be recognized as such, but they serve to introduce our argument.

To use rather more austere language, a heuristic is a simple and approximate rule—whether explicit or implicit, conscious or unconscious—that serves to solve a certain class of problems. Some banal examples of heuristics would be the way

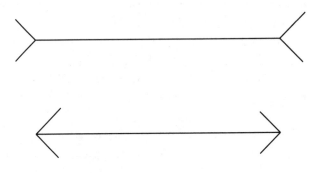

FIGURE 2

we think of objects that seem to us to grow smaller as they grow more distant, and objects that seem clear to us as close, whereas objects that appear dense and compact we consider to be heavy. The heuristic perception represented by the St. Louis arch, or by the famous two segments of a line known as the Müller-Lyer figure (Figure 2), is much more specialized.

To go beyond direct perception, we can easily recognize in ourselves more elaborate heuristics, such as "seeing" a number as even or odd by paying attention only to the last digit, or taking it for granted that a low-number license plate is a sign of influence or power. These are all, albeit very down-to-earth and close to the threshold of our consciousness, examples of cognitive heuristics. In fact, we don't make much of them, for they come to us spontaneously every day, and we are not even aware that we adopt them as heuristic strategies. But it doesn't take a moment's thought for us to become suddenly conscious of the existence or nature of these simple mental strategies.

There are, however, other cognitive heuristics that we all adopt spontaneously but that are exceedingly difficult to explain, even when they are specifically brought to our attention—as I now show.

A biologist assures us that there exists, in plants, insects, and human beings, an internal organ called the golgi. How likely is it, do you think, that a rabbit will also have a golgi, given that plants, insects, and humans have one? All of us are pretty certain that a rabbit, too, must have one.

The same biologist now informs us that both duck eggs and goose eggs contain biotine. How probable is it that a swan egg will also contain biotine? Here again, we feel pretty sure that a swan egg also contains biotine. Five-year-olds will answer just as we do. We know very little about the golgi (a semi-imagined organ stolen from biologists by cognitive scientists) or what biotine (a genuine vitamin, whose name is used by cognitive scientists for experiments in "spontaneous induction") is. What is more, we don't feel any *need* to know more to conclude that if plants, insects, and human beings have such an organ (of whatever sort), so must a rabbit, and that if the eggs of ducks and geese contain biotine, so *most probably* do the eggs of a swan.

Can we explain why? It is not difficult for adults (or even a child) to offer certain improvised justifications (the similarity among certain species, the uniform chain of living beings, and others) for these intuitive judgments. An important truth, however—which we call, after the philosopher who first pointed it out, the "Wittgenstein paradox"—is that we are no *more secure* of any of these principles, criteria, or general heuristics than we are of our own individual judgment. The rabbit, too, must have a golgi, because plants, insects, and we humans possess such an organ. We would bet with more certainty on this than we would on most any general principle that would embrace all living beings.

Here is the paradox. It is not logically possible to *justify* an intuitive judgment—delivered, as this one is, on an uncertain basis—on the basis of a general principle of which we are *less* certain. So how do we justify our judgments on the golgi and biotine? The fact is, our judgment is *not* justified. *It is correct, but it has no justification.* These are spontaneous judgments on which we are willing to bet, but that we could never justify rationally. No philosopher of science or psychologist could possibly build a serious justification (that is to say a *deductive* justification, deriving from first principles and worked out according to strict logic).

For such cases we have a powerful normative theory, known as the calculus of Bayesian induction (to which I return later). But in fact, Bayesian induction is *not* what we take into account in our *spontaneous* strategies. Our judgment on the question of the golgi or biotine (just two examples among many) is based on a heuristic, not on any rigorous procedure. Our judgment is, I insist, correct. A biologist could justify it empirically in *many* ways, but we formulate the judgment knowing nothing of the biologist's "reasons." We formulate it in rough-and-ready form, intuitively—in fact, heuristically.

We should know that one intrinsic characteristic of a heuristic is that it is *fallible*, and that it may be unjustified. A pound of feathers weighs exactly as much as a pound of lead; a miniature object can be both small and near; and as anyone who knows the sea is aware, a coastline may seem utterly clear in every detail but still be quite far away. We are all aware that our intuitions are fallible, but there are cases when we find it difficult to abandon our intuitive judgments. These are the most dangerous cases and we shall explore significant examples. The concept of heuristics embraces the examples we have just seen, and of course many others. Thus, despite its technical and somewhat unwieldy name, in real life it is utterly *central* to our everyday way of perceiving and thinking.

Let us turn to the notion of bias, which I have rather loosely tied to the idea of tunnels of the mind. In ordinary language we take this to mean a mix of prejudice, of partiality in our judgment, a slightly perverse inclination to be unjust without meaning to be so or to be extreme in our opinions. In short, the one word covers a multitude of blinders that we wear when (often without knowing it) we "look at" certain situations with our mind's eye. For brevity's sake, I continue to use the term *bias*, for it has also become a "technical" term in cognitive science.

Thus when our heuristics constantly draw all of us in a certain mental direction, when we are all brought to make the same mistake, then we can identify a bias in ourselves. Against its own will, our mind enters a tunnel in its reasoning. A pound of feathers weighs as much as a pound of lead? Well, which would you rather have fall on your head from the second floor? There's the bias. Our notion of weight is based on the idea of resistance, of solidity, of collapse, of how much *force* is needed to lift an object and how much damage that object can cause on impact.

Psychologists have measured this bias by constructing little cylinders of different sizes and asking people to make a rough-and-ready guess as to their weight. With the help of a scale, the psychologists concluded that what seems heavier to most of us is that which requires the greatest effort to lift or handle (even with just two fingers). Oddly enough, the scale is often not taken as authoritative. Our common, intuitive notion of weight is *inseparable* from the concept of physical force, of an object's compactness, its density, its hardness, its potential impact. To lift a pound of lead, which is tiny and can easily be handled with one hand, requires more concentrated muscular force than to lift a pound of feathers, which is larger and which we handle with two hands. As for the potential harm caused by a possible impact, the difference becomes drastic. *In this sense*, a pound of lead weighs more than a pound of feathers. When we take the former in our hand, we genuinely "feel" a concentration of force; we therefore assume that the object weighs more.

Our system of muscle commands, and our rapid analysis of what we feel (which we call proprioceptive), is not fashioned in such a way that we can compare, in a rough-and-ready way, the relative weights of a pound of lead and a pound of feathers. Suppose that we are asked to weigh carefully in one hand a pound of lead, and then just as carefully a pound of feathers, to which more feathers are added until we say "stop!" when we think the weight has reached a pound. In this case the margin of error can easily amount to more than half a pound, and many experiments prove that we make gross errors.

It remains difficult to say whether the bias here lies in our muscles or in our head. The answer is: probably a little in each.

The error is not, strictly speaking, cognitive, nor is it sensory (that is, proprioceptive). The mistake belongs to both worlds, without being completely worked out in either.

Generally speaking, since what is now known as the cognitive revolution, modern knowledge of the workings of the mind has shuffled the cards in regards to this traditional division between the cognitive and the sensory. For instance, in the world of language it is quite normal to invoke certain operations, representations, and abstract rules that are neither strictly "acoustic" nor "mental." That is, they take place neither in the ear nor in the brain, but astride both. Likewise, in other areas of cognitive science—such as in our sight or in the control of our movements—the traditional demarcation line between perception and mental processes no longer holds good. More important are certain specific aspects of problems, and certain very specific aspects of data inputting and formatting; these have replaced the traditional subdivision among the five senses, or the line between perception and thought or between what is closely related to the senses and what is proper to reasoning. The pages that follow show this.

With these premises in mind, we can right away have a look at a cognitive bias amply studied by Amos Tversky and Daniel Kahneman.

> A play is put on that Mr. Baker is most anxious to see. A ticket costs $100, and though Mr. Baker is not rich, he decides to buy two tickets. Now consider the two following situations:
>
> 1. Baker buys his two tickets a long time before the performance, but a week later his tickets have gone completely astray.
> 2. The day before buying his tickets, Baker realizes that there are $200 less in his bank account.
>
> How probable do you think it is that Baker buys another pair of tickets in case 1?
> How probable do you think it is that Baker will anyway buy a pair of tickets in case 2?

As most of us can readily guess, the dominant reply to this scenario is that it is *more probable* that Baker will buy two tickets in case 2 than that he will buy another pair in case 1. There is no economic rationality in this choice (for in both cases Baker is poorer by $200 and still has to spent another $200). The difference between the two cases is due to a psychological bias, which is known as "mental budget allocation." As cognitive scientists and economists who study the psychological foundations of negotiation well know—as does (at least implicitly) anyone used to making deals—all of us have a resistance to "overspend" a certain particular budget. In this case, the ticket budget would be overspent by Baker in the first scenario, but not in the second.

As if this were not perplexing enough, in this domain of mentally allocated budgets there also exists another, almost opposed, bias: a propensity to invest ever more, to bring to fruit a certain investment, *once we have irreversibly made that investment.* We are initially reluctant to overspend from a specialized mental balance (as is the case with Baker), but in other cases, once we have actually committed a large sum, we are inclined to add to it more than we would ever have accepted to spend at the beginning—if, that is, we think that this is the only way to make the initial investment bear some fruit.

Suppose Baker has bought the two expensive tickets, but on the evening of the much-awaited show there is a terrible snowstorm. The theater is far away, and Mr. and Mrs. Baker have to drive a long distance in the most uninviting circumstances. Actually, had they bought no ticket at all, they would *gladly* turn down an offer of $200 conditional on their acceptance to drive the same distance through the storm. In spite of this, surprising as it may seem, the likelihood is still high that they will go to the theater simply because they have spent $200 on the tickets. They would refuse the offer of $200, but they do not feel like wasting the *same* amount of money irretrievably congealed in the tickets. What makes the difference? Don't ask a pure economist, for he would detect none. But if you ask a cognitive scientist, he will tell you there is a significant difference, as we will see in the following chapters. The factors involved in many situations of this kind are called "sunk cost," "endowment effect," "asymmetry between gains and losses," and so on. Many interesting variants of these situations have been studied by the bright "impure" economist Richard H. Thaler of Cornell University. For instance, the "endowment effect" is the one also responsible for the fact that someone may well turn down an offer of $200 to sell two bottles of a rare claret he has bought a long time ago at a much lesser price, *and* equally flatly turn down the (hypothetical) offer to buy those two very bottles of claret for $200, if he did not own them already. (He surely does not intend to spend $200 to buy two more, a revealing fact, though, of course, this case is slightly different from the previous one—but revealing all the same.) The sunk-cost effect and the endowment effect, and various combinations thereof, have no place in a purely rational economic theory, yet it is through mental mechanisms of this kind that individuals, firms, and so-called sovereign states are brought to invest ever more on some investments that already have a long history when, should they be able to start again from scratch, they would not invest so much as a dollar.

The pure economic calculation and the cool calculation of risk are interpenetrated with psychological factors that have a decisive importance of their own, and also a foreseeable and calculable economic effect. *Both* the rigidity of "mental budget allocation" *and* the unlimited way in which "sunk costs" can be extended weigh on each and every one of us; so, too, does "regret," which prevents us from terminating investments and enterprises that carry a long freight of history and are full of hopes, disillusionments, economic projections, risks, and previous attempts to recoup.

These complex biases are especially carefully analyzed by economists and psychologists working on negotiations. Today there is a highly specialized branch of psycho-economics that works on these very processes, including the fairly universal phenomenon known as the "minimization of regret." We can all understand that our friend Mr. Baker feels greater regret for the $200 spent on his theater tickets and not put to use because of the storm than for the $200 not gained by refusing the offer to drive a distance in the snowstorm.

Other cases of regret are the following:

> For years, for so long in fact that he practically forgot he had them, Mr. Baker has owned $20,000 worth of shares in a certain company. One day he remembers them and considers whether it's worth hanging on to them or whether he should sell them. He notes that they have exactly maintained their value constantly over the years, so he decides to keep them— that is, to do nothing.
>
> A few months later, unexpectedly, the company fails and his shares are no longer worth a thing. He finds himself having lost $20,000.
>
> His friend, Mr. Jones, has also owned shares worth $20,000 in a certain company, and he, too, has all but forgotten he possessed them. One day, he remembers those shares, and considers whether he ought to keep them or whether he should sell them. He notes that they have exactly maintained their value throughout those years, so he decides to get rid of them and invest in a company that promises a greater return.
>
> His new investment, however, does not work out as well as Jones thought. Moreover, a few months later, that company whose shares he had sold unexpectedly markets a new product and the value of that company's shares doubles. Jones finds himself with $20,000 less than he might have had, had he not sold the shares he had kept for so many years.

Both started in the same position, and both came to an identical conclusion ($20,000 less), but Baker and Jones will not feel the same way. Which of them will suffer the greater regret? Clearly Jones will!

The reason that Jones's regret is greater than Baker's is that by Jones's action he altered a situation that had long worked neither to his advantage nor to his disadvantage, and he would have been better not touching it at all.

One of the most prevalent instances of a tunnel in the mind is to think that actions and decisions require a greater justification than inaction, than failing to decide, than leaving things as they are (especially if that has been the case for a long time). Our mental economy has a built-in cost for action. If our actions do not pan out, or cause a loss, we regret having acted. If, instead, we do not act, if we leave things as they are, and our investment does not pan out, or we lose, we still suffer regret, but the regret is *lesser*. Note, please, that these are not actions that require a determined effort. Baker and Jones buy or sell their shares via a perfectly ordinary telephone call. The cost of this sort of action is purely mental, not physical.

Here is another classic case of "regret" that does not involve making or losing money.

> Baker and Jones ride to the airport together, sharing the cost of their taxi. They are due for different flights that are due to leave at five o'clock. Baker is headed for Chicago, Jones for Los Angeles. The taxi gets stuck in an unusual traffic jam and doesn't arrive at the airport until 6:30. Jones's flight left on time, Baker's left an hour and 15 minutes late. Both have missed their flights, but whose regret is the greater?

You can be sure that Baker feels the greatest regret. To have missed a plane by a mere 15 minutes and not even know you were doing so, even if due to a delay for which you are in no way responsible, causes more regret than to lose by a full 90 minutes.

These have been a few simple and classical examples of strictly cognitive biases in the realm of economics, investment, and regret. I have noted them, after a few examples that related more closely to perception, to show in their full amplitude the concepts of heuristics and tunnels of the mind.

Before going on to look at other examples, let us dispense with one possible objection. It could be said, and not unreasonably, that these examples also carry a certain emotional freight (regret is an emotive state, as well as a cognitive one), and that therefore we cannot speak of pure cognition but rather must refer to a mixture of the cognitive and the emotive. Yet, the important fact is that these phenomena, and their cognitive causes, can perfectly well be "distilled" or separated out from their emotive correlates or consequences; they are almost universal, can be communicated to others, and always lead to the same mistakes. I don't think the cases of Mr. Baker and Mr. Jones have involved any real "emotion." But we very well understood how they felt, and we were equally able to foresee *correctly* their reactions and their choices. This is enough to guarantee that these are phenomena that can be usefully analyzed in terms of "pure" cognitive science, in a psychology, as cognitive science is sometimes half-jokingly described, "minus the emotions."

Our Spontaneous Intuitions: Angels or Demons?

L et us now turn to the expression *cognitive illusion,* and let's compare this fairly new and revolutionary term to the more traditional notion of a perceptual illusion, particularly an optical illusion. In the world of perception, an illusion is to reality what a fallacy is to reasoning: an argument that is not true but has the appearance of being so. There is always some truth in any illusion; there is always some persuasion in a fallacy. Our business is to distinguish between angels and devils.

Contemporary cognitive science has given us evidence of this new class of phenomena—new to science, though as old as humankind itself. The question is whether these should be classed with Necker's cube (Figure 3), the Müller-Lyer figure, and Escher's drawings or with perpetual motion, the philosopher's stone, Reagan's Star Wars, or the so-called socialist paradise. That is, they stand halfway between true and proper optical illusions and the kinds of utopias in which people want to continue to believe. On the one hand, cognitive illusions are truly, genuinely cognitive, and this is something new. On the

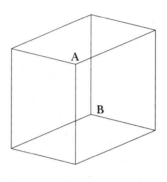

FIGURE 3

other hand, they are also truly, genuinely illusions, and this we can see by analyzing certain characteristics of classical perceptual illusions.

First of all, we have to recognize that a genuine illusion is not just an extravagance, an absurdity; it is something that always has some very plausible aspects. Likewise, a cognitive illusion is not an ordinary blunder; it does not originate in guesswork but from the formulation of a potent although mistaken intuitive judgment that, at least at first sight, convinces us within ourselves. It convinces us, but it also enters into conflict with other facts or other judgments, that are also compelling.

Another element crucial to every illusion is the weakness of our will. We may know perfectly well that the two lines in the Müller-Lyer figure are of equal length, but even after we've measured them one line *continues* to appear longer than the other. We may know perfectly well that the St. Louis arch (Figure 1) is *exactly* as broad as it is high. Yet, the truth is that our will does not control our eye; rational knowledge does not enter into our sense of visual organization. An optical illusion is the product of a low-level mental process, of the kind that is simple, rigid, stupid, specialized, and totally impervious to any intervention from a higher form of mentation, reason, or knowledge. In this sense, perceptual illusions and, though in a somewhat less striking way, cognitive illusions are a demonstration of what modern cognitive science calls the "modularity" of the mind. To use a somewhat exaggerated example, the organization of our mental modules more closely resembles the digestion of food than the meticulous preparation of a gourmet dish. In other words, it is more or less mechanical, as a computer is "stupid" for doing only what it's told to do.

The British psychologist Richard L. Gregory has come up with a trick (among many of his) that really ought to be seen in action, on videotape, but that I try to describe here in words. On a vertical panel of white plastic, two "sculpted" masks appear side by side. They are identical to each other except for a few details of illumination. When this panel is slowly turned (as though one were watching a door open), these two human faces turn away from each other, like two people who've had a quarrel and turn away slowly from each other. At a certain point in this movement, however, something quite incredible happens: While one of the two masks continues to turn on its path, the other one ceases to move, the whole mask collapses, and it is as though that head had rotated violently downward and then in the opposite direction to its former movement. This monstrosity is enough to turn one's head! But the trick is elementary and irresistible. What has happened?

Neurophysiologists have determined that, as monkeys have, our human brain has special receptors for human faces (or in the case of monkeys, for another monkey's face). These receptors consist of particular neurons activated *only* when they are presented with a face (a real one, or a photograph or a sculpture) in their field of vision. Gregory's trick takes advantage of these totally automatic receptors, which in turn combine with two other innate reflexes: one that always sees a face as protuberant toward ourselves and one that invariably sees a face as lit from above—that is, by the sun.

On Gregory's panel, one of the masks is concave (that is to say, it is recessed into the panel) and illuminated from below. When viewing this mask, one of our reflexes compensates for another, permitting our visual system to disregard these facts and to "see" the mask as protuberant and lit from above. The experiment with two masks cannot simply be depicted in still

The front of a hollow mask   *Partly rotated—so the hollow inside*
                                                starts to appear. (It looks hollow.)

FIGURE 4

(Photographs courtesy of Richard L. Gregory)

photographs, but something of the effect it demonstrates can
be seen in Figure 4, a mask of Charlie Chaplin as it is rotated.
As the mask turns we begin to see the inside, which is of course
concave, and yet once the mask has been fully rotated, we see
the face as protuberant.

In Gregory's two-mask experiment, as long as the mask
does not move, nothing contradicts our perceptual hypothesis.
I say "hypothesis" for a good reason, but it should be noted
that we have no cognizance of this fact at any conscious level.
When the mask turns, that part of our system of vision that is
ultraspecialized in regard to human faces persists in its error—
maintains its hypothesis and sticks with it to the end—seeing a
protuberant human face lit from above that turns in the opposite direction.

But there is a limit to everything, even to the rigidity and
the autonomy of a specialized component in our vision. At a

The hollow inside starts to look like a normal, nose-sticking-out, face— as more of its features appear.

Full-faced—hollow—but apparently normal face. It is hard to believe that this is a hollow mask—but it is!

FIGURE 4

certain point in the experiment with the two masks, as the rotation continues, the *real* play of light and shade makes the "hypothesis" (of a protuberant face lit from above) unsustainable, and the mask collapses as I described, because we suddenly see it as concave.

Believe me, though one knows every detail of this trick, the trap cannot be avoided; the phenomenon is irresistible. Reason cannot make the eye see differently.

I would like at this point to draw a few conclusions from these first examples.

- There exist in our nervous and mental systems certain circuits and computations that are autonomous, specialized, and by and large insensible to factors we know in other ways—by and large, but not totally. In fact, the hypothesis, protuberant and lit from above, collapses when the evidence against it becomes such as to render it psychologically and visually untenable.

- The revision of this instinctive hypothesis, unbeknownst to and impervious to the conscious mind, occurs in catastrophic form. To refer back to the Gregory masks, it is impossible for us to imagine a face that is, say 45 percent concave and lit from below or one that is 55 percent convex and lit from above. Our visual apparatus, and these "modules" in general, *start* from some simple hypothesis and end with another just as simple. There is nothing in between. As I've said, they're pretty stupid and totally impulsive. They do not behave like scientists (and like the other, nonmodular, intelligent, and rational components of our minds). They do not weigh different alternatives or measure their respective probabilities.

- The repertory of hypotheses available to a perceptual module is very limited, and as soon as one hypothesis is proved wrong, the module instantly goes to work on another.

- Nonetheless, though they are limited, autonomous, and ultrafast, no perceptual module (such as the one delegated to deal with human faces) is ever truly just an island. It interacts with other modules, such as with the module (equally automatic and innate) that makes us see a smooth and continuous trajectory in any rigid object in motion. That is why the mask seems to make a very rapid downward movement in the opposite direction to its previous movement. The sudden and discontinuous correction to the thesis "face protuberant, light from above" has likewise to cope with the *obligatory* continuity of trajectories, hence the system computes a lightninglike rotation of the mask downward and in the opposite direction.

I began by talking about there being the side of angels and the side of devils. Here we can see this very clearly. Angelic is a component that is able to make us reject a perceptual hypothesis that has become untenable and find another, contrary one. Diabolical, on the other hand, is the tenacity with which these modules hang on to a mistaken hypothesis until it becomes truly unsustainable. Demoniacal, too, is the illusory reconstruction of a continuous trajectory for the mask, disregarding the fact that this apparent motion is sudden, implausible, and totally unreal.

To understand better what is angelic and what is diabolical in our minds, we will soon have to move on to the mental meanderings of the most important cognitive illusions. The tunnels we are about to enter are a small but essential sample and, after all, my purpose is to give you a desire to make further voyages into our mental tunnels.

Let me therefore revert to the distinction I made earlier between "things that happen" and things we "do." So far, we have been talking about things that happen to us, such as the paradoxical movement of the Gregory masks and perceptual illusions in general. Among the things we do is the conscious elaboration of a hypothesis, the making of forecasts based on analysis, or seeking out a plausible explanation for certain facts.

It happens that in these high-level activities, cognitive illusions also exist, and things that "happen" infiltrate there, too: tunnel visions, or unrealized, impulsive, and rather stupid mini-reasonings that produce results very like those of the rapid and implausible rotation of the Gregory masks.

Let's take a brief example from logic, from that ancient and illustrious part of logic that involves syllogisms.

Given the premises:

All Ruritanians are rich;

John is a Ruritanian.

None of us will hesitate to come to the conclusion:

John is rich.

Even quite young children can cope with this sort of elementary syllogism.

Only a bit more difficult is the following:

Given the premises:

> *No fruit-picker is a sailor;*
>
> *All Ruritanians are fruit-pickers.*

One can logically deduce that:

No Ruritanian is a sailor.

Now try the following one on some of your most intelligent friends:

Given the premises:

> *All members of the cabinet are thieves;*
>
> *No composer is a member of the cabinet.*

What logical conclusion can we draw from this?

I've already stipulated that this should be put to the most intelligent, so that we don't get just ordinarily foolish answers, such as "No composer is a thief" or "No thief is a composer." Smart people will be careful not to offer such ill considered and illogical answers, or if they do, will immediately bite their tongues in shame.

Try it out for yourself. The answer you'll get from truly intelligent and thoughtful people is that *no* logical conclusion can be drawn from these premises. Almost without exception that is the answer you will get, after some serious reflection, from intelligent people. But, in fact, there is a conclusion to be drawn, just as incontestable as that offered by the two previous syllogisms. (I don't want to spoil your pleasure, so the correct answer is in "Tunnel Exits.") There is an answer, but *we don't see it* with our mind's eye.

The British psychologist Philip Johnson-Laird, currently a professor at Princeton University, has long studied this kind of reasoning and has produced a plausible explanation as to why we avoid the logical consequence of this particular syllogism. As you would expect, his explanation is psychological, not logical, because logic disregards whether a proposition is easy or difficult; it is only interested in whether it is *necessarily* true or *necessarily* false. A Martian might be somewhat surprised that we terrestrials find it so difficult to cope with this kind of syllogism. But the phenomenon is typically cognitive; it can only be explained psychologically. The pure logician can't cope with a concept such as "after serious reflection," or "most intelligent people," though these concepts are essential to the cognitive scientist. But these are curiosities of human nature; they are not logical.

Without getting into too great subtleties, Johnson-Laird's proposed solution turns on the number and complexity of the "mental models" each of us tacitly constructs to elaborate our reasoning on such syllogisms. The case of the cabinet ministers and composers requires—as the other two do not—three distinct, and mentally separate, arrays of obligatory couplings: cabinet ministers and thieves, composers and cabinet ministers, and thieves and composers. The result for all of us is a prohibitive difficulty in "seeing" that there are necessarily false couplings between thieves and composers. The correct conclusion is: *Some thieves are not composers.* Or, if you'd rather, *There are thieves who are not composers.* A full explanation is given in the section at the back titled "Tunnel Exits." Also, Johnson-Laird's book, appropriately called *Mental Models,* abundantly explains these arcanae of our spontaneous "logic."

The case of the unsuccessful syllogism leads us to a vital first lesson: that if even the most intelligent among us, even after the calmest and most attentive reflection, fall into this kind of mental tunnel, and over problems that *have* a strictly logical solution, imagine what happens to normal minds when they have to make quick decisions without complete information and at times when perhaps no one even knows whether a satisfactory answer *exists.* The tunnels that follow show what happens when we face a set of particularly interesting— because they are full of economic and social consequences—

problems. Here the question is our estimate of risk, our choices in betting or in lotteries, and, in general, our rough-and-ready estimates of probability.

Some of us who have already slipped into error will be upset as we show just how easily all of us are spontaneously and incorrigibly drawn into making huge errors, and precisely in situations where we cannot afford to do so: in clinical diagnoses, in court, in risky situations, and so on. Our final super-tunnel, the famous three-box problem, known as the Monty Hall paradox (see "Grand Finale") is probably the most striking and most famous example. A lot of ink has been spilled over it, and indeed, it made the front page of the *New York Times* and, when discussed in a popular science column, prompted literally thousands of letters.

Though the diffusion of the beginnings of an understanding of these mental tunnels has been slow, it has already had a certain influence on medicine, economics, the law, and even on the secret services. I do not hesitate to repeat what I said at the beginning: that these discoveries rank in importance alongside the discovery of the subconscious in psychoanalysis. For there exists, as we are beginning to see, a definite cognitive subconscious. The names of Amos Tversky (now at Stanford University) and of his long-time coauthor Daniel Kahneman (now at Princeton University, but for many of the most important early years of their collaboration both at the Hebrew University in Jerusalem) have such a prominent place in this area that it has become natural to talk of "Tversky-Kahneman" experiments. In Appendix A, I offer a brief history of this research.

Returning to the question of the angelic or the demonic, I would like to dispel any notion that humans are *necessarily* irrational animals. Irrational, and even exaggeratedly so, we frequently are, but not *necessarily*. The fact of the matter is that the demonic quality of cognitive illusions is always mitigated by the angel of reason. Those subjected to "Tversky-Kahneman experiments," which are problems that raise cognitive illusions, are often *conscious* that something is wrong with their reasoning.

This holds true for all: educated and ignorant, intelligent and stupid. They realize that something doesn't fit and pause to reflect on what's been said and thought.

However, only cognitive scientists and professional psychologists have been able to catalog these cognitive illusions, given them precise names, and understand exactly their nature (such things as anchoring, ease of representation, the law of small numbers, neglect of base rates, etc.). As our super-tunnel will show, anyone involved in one of these experiments or tests understands, in the intimacy of his reason, that something is tending to go awry. He may not know *what*, but he knows *something* isn't working. He doesn't need a psychologist to tell him that. But cognitive scientists and psychologists can now tell us exactly what is going on. Like Freudian analysts, they do no more than ask questions. On the sole basis of their questions, the subject understands *by himself* that his answers do not follow and that he is incoherent in his replies. Furthermore, he is often inclined (though not always, as the three-box problem will show) to reconsider his own intuitive judgment, and to change his mental strategies: that is, to seek a better heuristic strategy.

This feeling of unease and our switching to more effective heuristics indicate that we also are naturally predisposed to *force* ourselves into being rational. The discovery of the cognitive subconscious, therefore, is also an opportunity for us to rebuild our rationality on a more solid basis than those offered by classical psychology and traditional philosophy.

A clear example of this unease is the following: Many of us think there are more seven-letter words ending in -ing than there are with an "i" as the fifth letter (i.e., - - - - i - -).

The truth is that it is easier to *imagine* words ending in -ing than words that have an "i" as their fifth letter. But this notion is clearly a cognitive illusion. If one thinks for a moment, one realizes that every seven-letter word ending in -ing is an example of a word in which "i" is the fifth letter, so it is not possible for there to be more of the former than of the latter! Whoever *realizes* that she has been the victim of a cognitive illusion has no difficulty in admitting her error: that a subset cannot be larger than the set to which it belongs. Showing the two possibilities one after another, our sense of unease is clear. But if they are offered *separately*, to different people, this particular cognitive illusion shows up clear and strong. Not only that, but if the same person is asked about the two examples, a few days or weeks apart, with other tests intervening, she will fall into the same illusion. As you can see, human nature is a complex matter!

An analogous illusion makes us consider that there is a greater number of words beginning with an "r" than there are words that have an "r" in the third position. As the first group is infinitely easier to imagine (dozens of examples will occur to anyone immediately), our conclusion is that the first proposition must be true. In fact, there are vastly more words with an "r" in the third position than there are words that begin with an "r." Nonetheless, a vast majority of people consider that more words begin with an "r."

The opportunity cannot be missed here to reflect on an argument that I will be making later. It is central to the cognitive revolution, and it is that *our often-repeated experience of "how things are" does not serve to give us an accurate mental picture.* Every speaker of English has, during his lifetime, in newspapers, books, billboards, and ads, come across many more words in which an "r" appears three letters from the beginning, but this daily repeated experience is all for nought.

As Kant understood, the sieves built into our minds filter experience through their tiny apertures. We do not passively soak up forms and schemes from the external world, but manufacture our own internal constructions; we use in our way— that is to say, according to the nature of those sieves—only those things that serve to bring these filters to maturity. The fundamental root of our illusions, whether these be perceptual or cognitive, is the automatic application of such schemes to a reality that *could*, were it taken as it ought to be, *momentarily* falsify them.

In short, cognitive illusions are the product of the demon of mental facility (the technical term for which is *mental economy*)—that is, certain routine mental calculations, those that come to us with the greatest of ease and spontaneity and that seem so irresistible that we barely know we possess, use, or abuse them. That vague old concept "mental sloth" here takes on a scientific dignity. For reasons that I clarify later, some of these mental shortcuts just "happen" to us, whereas we explicitly and consciously adopt others, but without any justification worthy of the name. Many of the latter, perhaps because we are not conscious of adopting them, are probably innate (even if they manifest themselves later in life). As with the perception of faces in the Gregory experiment, they are mental "modules" that derive from how we are made, and not from our gender, our culture, our language, or our education. Cognitive illusions are of a small number of types that recur constantly; they all pull us in the same direction. We need only to offer slightly more refined problems, such as the three-box puzzle, to find even the greatest statisticians falling into the same trap.

On the other hand, our rational component is our guardian angel. It is that component that tells us something is awry and leads us to correct our mistakes in spontaneous judgment, and that component that *knows* how to come up with better answers. Sometimes, however, the demon wears angel's clothes. When that happens, spontaneous illusions become like rebellious angels. This occurs when we "don't listen to reason," when we manage to find ingenious, or pathetic, justifications for our erroneous reasoning. At that point we leave cognitive science and enter the domain of the psychopathology of personality. Our mental modules indeed interface with our emotional subconscious, with our ambitions and our jealousies, our pride and our superstitions. The fact that the cognitive unconscious is a separate and autonomous sector for our *studies* in no way precludes that in real people that unconscious in fact interacts with our feelings and our passions. Later on we will see some instances entirely symptomatic of that fact.

What cognitive science has admirably achieved is to distill these illusions into a state quite without emotive components. In real life, however, the two components are bound together. The verisimilitude always present in illusions, whether perceptual or cognitive, grows beyond measure. That partial impenetrability to reason of our mental tunnels now becomes a veritable rock wall.

Sometimes reason is enslaved; it is forced to collaborate— to protect our illusions, to render them immune to verification. At this point cognitive science stops as science and can only hope that the scientific study of cognitive illusions can someday find its complement in a true cognition of illusions, a form of science-cum-art that is able to integrate cognition and emotion. Toward that day there are the discoveries of Tversky and Kahneman, not to speak of those of Freud, but also those of Pirandello, Dostoyevski, Shakespeare, Van Gogh, and Wagner. While awaiting that day, let us prepare its advent by staying within the cognitive sciences.

A Brief Speleology of the Mind: An Easy Tunnel

Speleology is the scientific study of caves, and this chapter is an entre to the study of the "caves" of the mind or, as we will call them, mental tunnels. The example with which I begin has been verified on a large number of subjects. It is about rounding out numbers.

A subject is asked to multiply the following numbers in his head, and within five seconds:

$$2 \times 3 \times 4 \times 5 \times 6 \times 7 \times 8$$

Done? Good, write down the product on a piece of paper. Have a few other people try the same problem and note the results.

Now ask another set of friends, of the same age and level of intellect, to multiply the following, again within five seconds and in their heads:

$$8 \times 7 \times 6 \times 5 \times 4 \times 3 \times 2$$

Note the answers and enjoy the surprise. The average product of the multiplications in the second problem is not only different from that of the first, but also significantly greater.

Nonetheless, as has been demonstrated, when one asks these subjects individually to define the rule of commutation (that "changing the order of the factors does not alter the product"), the vast majority know the rule perfectly well. What happens is that, even though we know the rule, each of us undergoes an asymmetrical "rounding off" process in each of the two examples. The correct result is in "Tunnel Exits," and I'm willing to bet most of you find it very large, and in any event larger than the average of the products arrived at by mental arithmetic. This particular cognitive illusion is know as "anchoring," and we see more examples of it later.

In the example we have just seen, what happens is that we *begin* to calculate in our heads quite quickly, from left to right; when we run out of time we make a wild extrapolation of the rest. It is interesting that this extrapolation (an intuitive strategy that "imagines" what might be obtained if one "continued" multiplying *exactly*, with pencil and paper) remains *anchored* to the first product we obtain. We seem never to stray far from that—or never far enough. It is as though we were unable to forget our first estimate.

In the case of the ascending numbers, let's say we see that $2 \times 3 \times 4$ equals something like 20. We then extrapolate from that, having duly noted that the numbers get larger. Our extrapolation is high, but never high enough. On the average, that original product will be multiplied by 20, rather than by 2,000 as it ought to be. In the case of descending numbers, we do the same thing. We "see" that $8 \times 7 \times 6$ gives something like 400, and then we extrapolate from that, knowing that the numbers are getting smaller. Once again we stay "anchored" to our first product of 400, even when quadrupled, quintupled, or decupled. We don't multiply by 100, as we ought to. The differences between the two "anchor" figures account for the different replies and explain why there is so *consistent* an underestimate.

It would seem the time has come to revolutionize our old demarcation between things that we do and things that happen to us. This quick calculation is in fact something we "do." But the "anchoring" strategy is something that "happens" to us. So true is this that we are not even aware of its happening. We all realize that we are making an initial approximation and then extrapolating. But few of us are aware that we remain solidly and wrongly "anchored" to our first product. Another thing that happens to us, as we will see shortly in a paradigm example (Chapter 4, Tunnel 1), is that we are "trapped" in each case by the order that is presented to us. Very few subjects in fact spontaneously reverse the order of numbers in working out either version of the problem. Although both mental calculations give an estimate significantly lower than the true value, thus preserving the anchoring effect, it nonetheless would be revealing to witness that we obtain two *different* estimates. It would, if we did this sort of mental reversing, but we don't. Hardly ever do we spontaneously alter the formulation of a problem that is presented to us in a reasonably clear and complete way. This form of mental sloth is what the "framing" effect is all about. One accepts the problem as it is presented and few subjects think of reformulating it in an equivalent but different manner. We don't, for instance, reverse the order of the numbers, though we know perfectly well that the result should be identical. We know that, but we don't *use* our knowledge in a situation when clearly to do so would be relevant, and, in the case of the ascending order, even helpful, though not decisive.

Here then is an elementary example of a mental tunnel: something present in another corner of the mind that is known (commutation) but in many cases remains inaccessible. Our estimate of the product fails to use a tool that we possess and that clearly would be helpful. We only understand how helpful when we emerge from our little mental tunnel. As long as we stay in that tunnel, our intuition remains an unwitting and strange mixture of things we do and things that happen to

us, a combination of explicit calculation and compulsive intuition, of reason and unreason.

This is typical of many cases. Data and procedures that are
in theory accessible, and that we can show we have stored away
in some corner of our minds and therefore should use, in fact
remain unaccessed. It is as though some inherent mental barrier kept us from reaching other areas of the brain. Hence the
use of the term *tunnel.*

Luckily, we are neither moles nor full-time speleologists.
Something happens to us, other data filter through, and the
problem is *somewhat* modified or radically reformulated; our
mental itinerary changes, and then that other area is as though
miraculously available to us. In modern cognitive science,
these are what we call "heuristics" and "biases." Now that we've
seen them at work on very basic problems, let's pass to some
deeper and more interesting tunnels.

C H A P T E R   4

Probability Illusions

I have just tossed a coin 7 times, and I ask you, who have not seen the result, to guess which of the three sequences below represents the sequence of my results. I guarantee that one of the sequences is genuine. If you don't get it right, you lose 10 dollars; if you win, you get 30. H stands for heads, and T for Tails.

1. **HHHHTTT**
2. **THHTHTT**
3. **TTTTTTT**

On which would you bet? Let's think for a moment before going on.

Experiments with a great many subjects have shown that the bets will be placed in the following order: 2, 1, 3. The preference for the second sequence is very strong. But probability theory tells us that in seven tosses of a coin the probabilities are totally even, and we rationally should be quite indifferent to which of the three sequences we choose. The person who chooses 2 is prey to one of the most common cognitive illusions: she mistakes the most *typical* for the most *probable*.

It is worthwhile underlining here that our spontaneous, wild guesses as to what is "typical" show up in the world of probability and play on us some nasty tricks. The vast majority of ordinary mortals don't have the foggiest idea of the precise definitions and the rigorous calculation proper to probability. Yet somehow each thinks he knows—typicality is what gives us this illusion of knowing.

Here is another, more complex, example of a probability illusion, this one more interesting:

> A normal die has been painted in such a way that it has four green faces and two red. After being shaken in a cup, the die is thrown repeatedly onto the table, and the reader is invited to guess which of the following sequences represents the actual one. Once again, it is stipulated that one of the three is the real one, and the bet is the same: it will cost you 10 dollars if you get it wrong, and you get $30 if you get it right. (R is for red and G is for green.)

1. RGRRR
2. GRGRRR
3. GRRRRR

On which do you bet? Think.

The preferences usually expressed are, in order, 2, 1, 3. You will note that the likelihood of throwing green is four out of six, or two-thirds, whereas that of getting red is two out of six, or one-third—twice as unlikely. The sequences offered to the subjects are all heavily unbalanced toward the (more unlikely) red, and many subjects explain that sequence 2 is somehow more "balanced," or less unbalanced, and *therefore* more probable. Here is another case in which the "typical" seems more likely.

What is more extraordinary is that some 65 percent of all subjects (exception made of expert statisticians and people whose business is probability) show a strong propensity to vote for sequence 2, even when it is explicitly pointed out that one can obtain sequence 1 from sequence 2 just by eliminating the first throw of the die. Even the most elementary notion of probability ought to tell us that the chances of the longer sequence being correct (because of the additional throw of the die) are two-thirds fewer. In fact, the probability of a "global" event that is composed of several independent events is given by multiplying the probabilities of the component events. Whatever the probability of 1, the probability of 2 is obtained by multiplying the probability of 1 by the probability of getting green in an *additional* throw—that is, by two-thirds. The firm-footed intuition here should be that, by adding another throw to a series, to *any* series, I obtain a "larger" event that is, at best, less probable than the "smaller" event by a factor of two-thirds (if I bet on an additional green) and at worst by a factor of one-third (if I bet on an additional red). Notwithstanding this simple and obligatory consideration, 2 still seems a more "balanced" sequence, and therefore more probable. This is the cognitive illusion that leads most of us to prefer 2 to 1, which seems less balanced. Tversky and Kahneman call this the "law of small numbers." In contradistinction to the probability calculus, which is based on the law of large numbers, our intuition expects to find the "norm" of alternation of aleatory (or "chance") results respected even in very brief sequences.

This illusion is also known as the "gambler's fallacy." If at roulette red has come up 20 times in a row, we will bet on black, even though the chance remains only one in two, regardless of whatever occurred earlier. The gambler's fallacy is to believe that in a brief sequence of genuinely chance events, sooner or later (or as he believes, sooner rather than later), the equilibrium between red and black will be reestablished at about 50 percent. *Statistically, we believe something to be true for short sequences that is only approximately true for very long sequences, and rigorously true only for sequences near to infinity.*

In the case of the coins—banal, but no less interesting for that—statistics show that not only is each of the three sequences equally probable, but also that *any* sequence of tossed coins is as likely as any other. The idea that "alternating" heads or tails are more likely is only an illusion. The mathematical laws of probability have an objective measure to show that this is an illusion. Things may appear one way subjectively, but really they are quite different from what they seem.

The case of the die is slightly more complex, but the illusion remains clear and strong; it also persists when the subject's attention is drawn to the fact that two of the sequences are such that one "dominates" the other (that is, *whatever* the probability of the one, the likelihood of the other is *necessarily* lesser). In fact, as we just saw, the probabilities of individual throws in *any* sequence must be multiplied to obtain the probability of the sequence as a whole. The longer the sequence, the less probable it is, *independently* of its being "balanced" or "unbalanced." This shows how resistant certain cognitive illusions are. Many other more complex examples have been advanced, and these show that even professional statisticians are sometimes subject to the same illusion.

Mental Tunnels

With these first timid excursions under our belt, let us now take up some far deeper tunnels.

Tunnel 1: The Framing of Choices

We begin with a sort of classic of the genre known as the "framing of choices."

> Imagine that the United States is preparing for the outbreak of an unusual Asian disease that is expected to kill 600 people. Two alternative programs to combat the disease have been proposed. Assume that the exact scientific estimates of the consequences of the program are as follows:
>
> If Program A is adopted, 200 people will be saved.

If Program B is adopted, there is a one-third probability that 600 people will be saved and a two-thirds probability that no people will be saved.

Which of the two programs would you favor?

Think about it for a moment, and make your choice. The preference expressed by a majority of subjects is in "Tunnel Exits."

This same test, in somewhat different form, was given to another set of subjects, in all respects equal to the first set. The formulation in that test is as follows:

Imagine that the United States is preparing for an outbreak of an unusual Asian disease that is expected to kill 600 people. Two alternative programs to combat the disease have been proposed. Assume that the exact scientific estimates of the consequences of the program are as follows:

If Program C is adopted, 400 people will certainly die.

If Program D is adopted, there is a one-third probability that no one will die and a two-thirds probability that 600 people will die.

Which of the two programs would you favor?

Though presenting both versions, as I am forced to do here, one right after the other is not the right way to go about it, I again suggest that the reader reflect carefully and then make her choice. The framing effect is so robust and widely diffused that even in this rather crude form it will still be effective. Once again, the choices expressed by a majority of subjects are found in "Tunnel Exits."

Rational decision making would indicate that, in a sense, we should be *indifferent* not only to the choice between A and B, or between C and D, but also to *all four of these possibilities.* I say "in a sense" because there is an abstract magnitude that remains exactly the same in all four choices: what is called "expected value." A minimum of reflection will convince you that there is a calculation that would make these four options perfectly equivalent. This calculation (which has little, if any, psychological appeal, but which we know scientifically is a very relevant one) says that we can usefully multiply the "gain" or the "loss" by the probability of attaining one or of having to pay for the other. The basis of this calculation (of the expected value) is that a $1,000 prize with a probability of 50 percent is "worth" $500. Psychologically, of course, it isn't so, because we naturally prefer the certainty of a lesser sum over the uncertainty of a larger sum. Moreover, when large sums are at stake, an increase in the objective monetary value of the stakes does *not* match, dollar for dollar, an increase in what they are worth *for us*. As the fathers of probability calculus, and then the founders of modern economics and decision theory, have discovered, subjective "utility" does not parallel objective "value." The curve of subjective utility "flattens out" as true dollars rise. In simple words, and taking an extreme case, the subjectively perceived "utility" for me of getting a million dollars, judged from my present financial situation, is vastly greater than the *difference* between getting 15 million and getting 16 million dollars. In pure monetary terms, the stakes are the same: 1 million dollars more. Yet, it is a plain fact for all of us that the effect each of us is ready to deploy to make it vaguely possible to win a million is much higher than the *additional* effort one would deploy in order to make it vaguely possible to win 16, rather than 15, million. What applies to sums that we are sure to win, or lose, also applies to sums we may win, or lose, with a certain probability. The flattening out of the subjectively estimated "worth" (called subjective utility) and the special subjective appeal of certainty over uncertainty (even over very, very slight uncertainty) must be accounted for when we build up a modern, psychologically realistic theory of decisions. Barring extreme cases, one surely would *not* want to condemn this flattening out of subjective utilities, and the appeal of certainty over uncertainty, as "irrational."

A very rich person will probably have a rating of subjective utilities different from a very poor person, but there are interesting and effective ways of *abstracting away* from personal idiosyncracies in these matters. The curve of the rich will be numerically different from the curve of the poor, but they will both flatten out as stakes rise (they are both concave toward rising monetary values, as it is said in the jargon). The *form* of the curve is, so to speak, universal. Therefore, modern decision theory is centered around "expected utilities," not "expected values." It allows us to calculate what is, and what isn't, rational, *given* the flattening out of expected utilities. Moreover, an important conceptual link exists between the two. If we play heads or tails for $10, the "just" (or "fair") price of this bet, what we should reasonably stake, is $5. If we bet on a single die, and the stake is $6, the fair price is $1, for only one face can win. The fair price is the one for which it is rational *in the abstract* to remain indifferent between accepting the bet and refusing it. From the point of view of expected value, if you are offered this bet for less than the fair price, then it is irrational to refuse it. If, on the contrary, you are offered this bet for more than the fair price, then it is irrational to accept it. But we have to reconsider the situation also from the (quite different) point of view of expected utility. The situation might well be one in which it would be irrational for you to accept the bet at *any* price. (Suppose that $1 is all you have in your pocket and you have to make a very important phone call, or you have to use it to buy your bus ticket back home.) Moreover, a certain individual may well be unwilling to accept any bet, ever, under any circumstance. Again, we would not want to dub this person as "irrational." Let's suppose, however, that we are not in any of these special and somewhat extreme situations, and proceed to develop a suitably general theory of rational decisions taking into account (in ways we do not have to go into here) *both* expected value *and* expected utility. Let's now continue with the case of our deadly disease.

Applying the calculation of expected value (the hard-line, dispassionate, psychologically rather "inhuman" way to pro-

ceed) to our epidemic, all four proposals have an equal expected value: 200 lives saved. Our failure to "see" this equivalence, not to sense the fact that the choice is statistically
(though not psychologically) indifferent, has nothing "irrational" per se, but paves the way to another of our tunnels, the
one we call "the framing of choices." What *is* irrational, in
terms of expected *utilities* (the good count, the psychologically
applicable one), is to express preferences in the domain of
losses (lives lost) that are at odds with the preferences expressed in the domain of gains (lives saved). Our problem here
is that we do not compute final "assets" (so to speak), but only
departures from a baseline. The two formulations make us compute a different baseline, and we end up with conflicting final
preferences. From the point of view of expected utilities, there
is nothing wrong with preferring A to B. However, once you
have chosen A, you *ought* to choose C, not D. In fact, aside from
the way it is described (or, one would want to say here,
"framed"), C is exactly the same "state of the world" as A. And
the same objective (though not psychological) equivalence
holds between B and D. We are witnessing here that we are
indeed trapped in one of our mental tunnels. In the more
"benign" and psychologically "tolerant" theory of decisions,
the one based on expected utilities (not expected values), what
is irrational is to prefer A to B *and* D to C.

The Asiatic epidemic may not seem very realistic, but the
"framing" error has been the subject of many far more concrete, and therefore more alarming, tests. In 1982, McNeil,
Pauker, Sox, and Tversky submitted a selected, but revealing
sample of U.S. doctors to a test that was qualitatively very similar, but was based on actual clinical data. They showed that a
significant majority of these clinicians were subject, as we are,
to the "framing" error. If they were told that there was a mortality rate of 7 percent within 5 years for a certain operation, they
hesitated to recommend it; if, on the other hand, they were
told it had a survival rate after 5 years of 93 percent, they were
more inclined to recommend it to their patients. It's like the
old question of whether the glass is half empty or half full. A

mortality rate of 7 percent is a glass half empty, but a survival rate of 93 percent is a glass half full. It shouldn't make any difference, but it does.

Even when we become professionals, this sort of framing error works away within our minds. The authors published their disconcerting results in the prestigious *New England Journal of Medicine*, and the medical profession had to pay attention to the results of cognitive science. In fact, for a number of years now, some medical schools in the United States and in Israel regularly include classes on these omnipresent aspects of "bias" that play so important a part in diagnosis.

Tunnel 2: Segregating Decisions

"Framing" is governed, in large part unconsciously, by two spontaneous rules: acquiescence (technically called, in a somewhat less vivid word, "acceptance") and segregation. We can think of these as rules of "mental economy," which we can translate as "mental sloth," because that is indeed what underlies them. Acquiescence means that when we are faced with a reasonable formulation of a problem involving choice, we accept it in the terms in which it is formulated and do not seek an alternative form. In other words, we will always seek to solve a problem *as presented*. Thanks to our cognitive sloth (not because we seek to shirk), we become prisoners of the frame we are offered. Cognitive scientists, in their experiments, quite knowingly offer us this one and only frame, but the effect is not only seen in experiments. Real life offers us, day in and day out, many instances of our incapacity to shift the way a problem is presented to us and then maybe arrive at a "fresh" and more rational decision.

The reason we get trapped in acquiescence is closely connected with the second rule of mental sloth, which Tversky and Kahneman called "segregation." We isolate the problem from its global context; the problem itself becomes the immediate and exclusive center of our attention. We do not take into account all the pros and cons of our choice and its consequences. Having narrowly considered only the choices offered us, rather than considering the various global possibilities or probabilities available, we stare at our navels. In myopic fashion we take up *only* those actions and solutions that have an *immediate* effect on the situation, and always as they have been framed for us.

Here is a striking example of the combination of these two factors adapted from Tversky and Kahneman:

> First we are offered a bonus of $300. Then, we are asked to choose between the two following possibilities:
>
> A. To receive $100 for sure; or
>
> B. To toss a coin. If we win the toss, we will get $200; if we lose, we receive nothing at all.

Most of us (as Tversky and Kahneman show) prefer A to B. But the preference is inverted when another set of choices is offered.

> First, we are offered a bonus of $500. Then, we are asked to choose between the two following possibilities:
>
> C. We are guaranteed to lose $100; or
>
> D. We toss a coin, and if we lose, we have to pay $200, but if we win, we don't have to pay anything.

Here, the majority prefers D to C. These spontaneous choices seem perfectly "obvious" to us. But, were we not victims of segregation, reason and the laws of probability would tell us that we should be utterly indifferent as to our choice, whether between A and B, or C and D, or any one of the four choices. At the end of any one of these four games, the probabilities are rigorously similar: We should wind up with $400 more than we had when we started. Instead, we focus on each set of choices: we segregate each set from the overall picture—the situation *before* the test and that which prevails after the test, whatever choices we make.

Besides segregation, another bias is involved here. When considering a choice between certainty and probability, we are differently affected when the choice is presented as one of winning or when it is a question of losing. *We are spontaneously conservative when it comes to winning, and adventurers when we face loss.* Let's look a little closer, and a bit more mathematically, at this fundamental asymmetry between winning and losing.

It is quite true that in B above there is a 50 percent chance of winding up with $500 rather than $400, and that in D there is a 50 percent chance of winding up with $300 rather than $400. The reader will recall that the theory of expected value requires us to multiply the premium, or the penalty, by the probability of obtaining a sum or losing one. In B, a one-in-two chance (50 percent) of gaining an additional $200 gives us a value of $100 ($200 multiplied by one-half.) Therefore a 100 percent sure $100 is *equivalent* to $200 that we have a 50 percent chance of obtaining.

The same is true for a certain loss of $100 as against a 50 percent chance of no loss at all, or a 50 percent chance of losing $200. According to the theory of expected value and the laws of probability, there is no qualitative difference between gain or loss. All there is, mathematically speaking, is the substitution of a plus for a minus. The calculation, therefore, is exactly the same. When we compute, instead, expected utilities, we have to allow for the famous "flattening out" (or concavity) of the curve, but the standards of decision theory *still* have to assume that this curve is *the same* for gains and for losses. It flattens out, so to speak, in the same way for gains and for losses. At least that's what one would have said from a purely theoretical point of view. That's what the curve "ought to" do. In our case, what should count is the difference between the initial situation and the end of the game. In the choice between A and B (both of which offer a gain) we received an initial bonus of $300, whereas in C and D (both of which offer loss) we have received an initial $500. Thanks to segregation, we pay no attention whatsoever to this capital difference. We segregate the choice from its global context.

But that's not all. As many other tests show, when money is bet in what is called a "choice between lotteries," there is a vast *qualitative* difference when the choices offered are of winning compared to a choice between possible losses. We are "risk-seekers" when it comes to losses and "risk-averse" when we might gain. The powerful asymmetry shown in the choice of A over B (we bet on certainties when it comes to gain) but in choosing D over C (we will bet on uncertainties when facing loss) is a striking example. The curve of subjective utilities is qualitatively different for gains and for losses—a perplexing and very important result that finds no rational justification in the standard theory of choices. In short, when it comes to receiving, better the bird in the hand than the bird in the bush, but when it comes to losing, we prefer to *perhaps* have the bird in the bush rather than *certainly* have the bird in hand. Whoever's had to handle taxation matters (especially in my own country) knows this powerful difference, and is aware of the love of risk shown by those who gladly prefer to pay *maybe* several birds in the bush, than surely one out of the hand, here and now.

Key experiments that demonstrate our fear of risk when it comes to gain and our love of risk when we might lose have been conducted by Tversky, Kahneman, and their associates in recent years. (A first typical experiment was designed and carried out in the early 1950s by the French economist and Nobel laureate Maurice Allais.)

In the Tversky and Kahneman experiment, the subject is asked to imagine to have to choose between:

A. A sure gain of $75 and

B. A lottery in which there is a 75 percent probability of winning $100 and a 25 percent probability of winning nothing at all.

A substantial majority choose A over B. But as should by now be obvious, the subjective estimate of "expected utility" changes dramatically when we offer a similar choice between losses. To be precise, preference for the certain over the uncertain is reversed when subjects are asked to choose between:

C. A sure loss of $75, and

D. A lottery in which there is a 75 percent probability that we will lose $100 and a 25 percent probability of not losing anything.

Now D is preferred to C.

Once again, according to the disembodied and rather inhuman calculus of expected values, one should be indifferent between A and B, and then (separately, of course) between C and D. In the more humane, and more interesting, calculus of "expected utility" we are happy to acknowledge that the increase of $30 between $70 and $100 is a little less valuable to us than $30 would be if taken alone, that is, having zero as a reference point or, as professionals call it, as our *status quo*. We can also accommodate the preference of the certain for the uncertain, or at any rate allow for considerable slack in the personal propensities of different individuals to accept bets of any sort. What cannot be rationally endorsed, even in this more relaxed and more humane approach to rational decision making, is that the same individual, in the same moment of time, *both* prefers A to B *and* D to C. This is incongruous and contradictory. The steep asymmetry of our actual (not rational) personal curves of estimated utility (a sharp drop for losses and a mild climb for gains) is what explains these choices. It is a fact about us that we carry this curve in our minds, something that economists ought to pay attention to when studying the economic behavior of real human beings in a real world. It is a property of our psyche, but it cannot be licensed by any decent theory of rational choice.

Thanks to a series of experiments, Tversky, Kahneman, and their collaborators have been able to calibrate the asymmetry between these two opposing tendencies. Another good example, just as rigorous mathematically, is the following:

Betting takes place at two separate tables. At each table a coin is tossed. Here are the prizes offered by each table:

Table A: If you win the toss, you get $20; if you lose, you pay $5.

Table B: If you win the toss, you win X number of dollars, but if you lose you pay $15.

An auction is held, with sealed bids. What is the least you would bid to be given the opportunity to choose between Table A and Table B? Obviously, if you are too exacting—that is, if you bid too high for X—someone less demanding will win the bid and the right to play at Table B.

Consider your bids carefully. What would you bid to be given the opportunity of playing game B rather than game A? Note that in B there is a 50 percent chance of losing $15, whereas at Table A there is an identical probability of losing $5. The question, then, refers to how much greater the possible win should be to compensate for the greater possible loss. A little demon may now be whispering to you that a factor of three should somehow intervene. The average figures reported by Tversky and Kahneman after testing a variety of subjects are quite different (see "Tunnel Exits"). You will note that the average *minimum* sum offered by a large sample of subjects is clearly greater than the difference between the two possible losses. In other words, to accept the risk of a greater loss, we require a *large* increase in our possible (though not certain) winnings. A purely abstract rational calculation, based on expected value, and a psychologically more realistic one, based on our "expected utility" (with due concavity and all), would both lead us to be considerably less exacting in our demands. The psychological bottom line, however, is that we have in our minds a curve of expected utility that "dips" *much faster* in the domain of losses than it climbs in the domain of gains. We care a lot about this subjective, not rationally defensible, estimate of utilities, but little about rationality. The great advantage of this sort of experiment is that it enables us to put an exact dollar value on how little we care.

What is truly instructive, however, is the comparison with this other, perfectly analogous, test.

> Betting takes place at two different tables. At each table a coin is tossed. Here are the respective bets (all are now winning bets) offered by the two tables:

> Table C: If heads comes up, you win $15; if tails, you win $40;

> Table D: If heads comes up, you win $5; if tails, you win Y.

> Again, there is a silent auction with sealed bids. What is the minimum sum Y you would offer in your envelope for the chance to choose Table D over Table C? Here again, if you are too demanding, and ask too high a price for Y, someone else will win the bid and the right to play at Table D.

The reader is invited to make his *minimum* bid. Note that in the second case everyone wins; there is no possible loss.

The results of this test are given in "Tunnel Exits" (Tunnel 2). What is noteworthy is that when there are only wins, and no losses, the compensation required is *greatly less* than in the previous test. What this shows is that there is a considerable degree of psychological asymmetry between the prospect of winning and the prospect of mixed results (that is, some wins and some losses). This may seem entirely obvious, because such is human nature, but classical decision theory offers no such asymmetry. To be sure, in classical theory losses are indicated by a minus sign, whereas gains are marked by a plus sign, and both have the famous concavity of diminishing subjective values as stakes are raised, but both are governed by the same equations and the same principles of optimization. A rational theory sees no qualitative difference between winning and losing. Does that mean we should get rid of this theory? Unfortunately, we cannot do so, because certain fundamental mathematical theories hold that *only* a rational theory can, with any *certainty*, protect us from senseless wagers in situations such as the ones of Dutch bookies (see "Introduction"). If we follow our own impulsive strategies, and make our choices based on our own psychological makeup, then nothing can protect us in certain situations from being a cash pump for our adversaries. That is why science does well to study in depth *both* branches of our decision-making process: the "normative" rule (that is, those we should follow) and the descriptive rule (those we spontaneously do follow).

Tunnel 3: The Conjunction Effect

We are given a brief fact sheet. In quasi-telegraphic style, it describes the character and attitudes of Bill:

> Bill is 34 years old. He is intelligent, but unimaginative, compulsive, and generally lifeless. In school, he was strong in mathematics but weak in social studies and humanities.

On the basis of this very sketchy profile, we are asked to guess the likelihood that Bill exercises a particular trade or profession rather than another. Most important, we are asked to rank, in order of decreasing probability, a list of jobs and hobbies, amongst which are the following cases:

> Bill is a doctor, and his hobby is playing poker.
>
> Bill is an architect.
>
> Bill is an accountant. (A)
>
> Bill plays jazz for a hobby. (J)
>
> Bill surfs for a hobby.
>
> Bill is a reporter.
>
> Bill is an accountant who plays jazz for a hobby. (A & J)
>
> Bill climbs mountains for a hobby.

The reader is invited to hazard her own estimate of Bill, reordering these characteristics in descending order of probability. It is part of the rules of the game that our valuation of

Bill will be vague and approximate, a sort of rule-of-thumb. Precise values are not called for, only an intuitive general ranking of the relative likelihood of the above possibilities.

Let's now pass to another case study, analogous to the one above:

> Linda is 31 years old, single, outspoken, and very bright. She majored in philosophy. As a student, she was deeply concerned with issues of discrimination and social justice, and also participated in antinuclear demonstrations.

As with Bill, we are invited to guess what Linda's profession is, and to list, in descending order, the likelihood of each of the professions or hobbies below:

> Linda is a teacher in elementary school.
>
> Linda works in a bookstore and takes yoga classes.
>
> Linda is active in the feminist movement. (F)
>
> Linda is a psychiatric social worker.
>
> Linda is a member of the League of Women Voters.
>
> Linda is a bank teller. (T)
>
> Linda is an insurance salesperson.
>
> Linda is a bank teller and is active in the feminist movement. (T & F)

Again, the reader is invited to come up with an approximation and to list the above likelihoods in decreasing order.

Let her throw the first stone who has not picked A & J ahead of J for Bill, or T & F ahead of T for Linda.

That is what almost all of us do, though again this is a pure cognitive illusion. In fact, the likelihood that *two* of these characteristics should be simultaneously true (that there is what scientists call a "conjunction") is *always* and *necessarily* inferior to the probability of any one of the two characteristics taken alone. If you think for a moment, you will be obliged to admit that it *must* be more likely that Bill enjoys playing jazz while working at whatever (or at nothing at all, for case J in fact specifies nothing more than that he plays jazz as a hobby) than it is that he both plays jazz and is an accountant. The same is true for Linda. It has to be more likely that Linda is a bank teller and takes part in some movement or other (case T, in fact, specifies nothing more than that) than it is that Linda is both a bank teller and is an active feminist. Nonetheless, the vast majority of people submitted by Tversky and Kahneman to a huge gamut of tests think the conjunction more likely than one of the paired activities.

In fact, the average hierarchy surmised by our subjects is:

for Bill, that A is more probable than A & J, which in turn is more probable than J; and

for Linda, that F is more probable than T & F, which in turn is more probable than T.

What is really surprising is that there is no great difference in the average responses from the "uninformed" subject (that is, one who has no real notion of the laws of probability) and those of statistical experts. There is in fact a slight difference between the two groups: those who know something about statistics make more errors than the uninformed and also more than the experts. Even the experts, in fact, err more than the uninformed. The precise data for this experiment are in "Tunnel Exits."

Changing the nature of the problem offered, Tversky and Kahneman have been able to show that this bias, known as the conjunction effect, is just as common among doctors, generals, politicians, and engineers—*even in tests that relate to their specific area of expertise.* For instance, with a very similar form of test, it has been shown that a doctor is likely to consider the simultaneous presence of two normally associated symptoms (e.g., migraine and nausea) *more* probable than the presence of either of them separately. Similarly, military personnel and politicians will make a like mistake in the "Polish crisis" (see Chapter 7). This conjunction error is, in fact, one of the most widespread cognitive illusions. That should give us cause for concern.

The question is, what happens to us? Is it possible that more than 80 percent of us, including experts in statistical probability, make the same stupid mistake?

Some readers may have, for some time now, come up with an explanation that might *seem* to justify the conjunction error. This hypothesis is probably like the one that some psychologists advanced (some of them quite vehemently) when Tversky and Kahneman first presented their findings. This hypothesis is that the results observed could be due to *a set of linguistic misunderstandings*. In option J, for instance, the subject of the test could have thought that Bill's hobby is jazz, but he is *not* an accountant, or that, in option T, Linda is a bank teller, but she is *not* an active feminist. The doctor, when she considers a headache alone, might make the mistake of thinking that she has to take into account the likelihood of a migraine without nausea. And so on.

According to these critics, this is how the conjunction effect occurs. When one of the two occurrences is presented by itself, we take it as *implicit* that the other occurrence is *excluded*. In other words, we take "silence" about the second occurrence as a tacit exclusion or negation. Because option T says that Linda "is a bank teller," whereas option T & F says that she "is a bank teller and is active in the feminist movement," we take T to mean implicitly that she "is a bank teller, but is *not* (also) an active feminist." That, say these critics, is how the subjects receive the message, and that is how these critics seek to explain the inappropriate "ranking" of options.

If this criticism were true, given Bill's or Linda's "profile" (or in the case of the doctor, the combination of migraine and nausea), we would have to conclude that it is judged more likely that a certain *complex* of facts occurs than just one fact without the other. This would mean, as some readers have no doubt already concluded in their heart of hearts, that the test has been badly framed. If the test were "fair" linguistically, there would be no such thing as a conjunction effect and we wouldn't have to worry our heads about it. But is this objection legitimate?

No, it doesn't work. It will be noted first that the "ranking" offered by the vast majority of those taking the test indicates that the *most probable* of the three cases is precisely one in which only *one* of the two possibilities is true. Our incriminating conjunction, that is A and J for Bill and F and T singly for Linda, is, in fact, placed *higher* (judged more probable) than one of the two single "conjoined" possibilities (that is, it dominates one of the components of the conjunction in the scale of probabilities) but *lower* than the other (that is, it is in turn dominated by the other single "conjunct," in other words the probability of a single occurrence). If we really felt that this "silence" in the formulation of cases A, J, F, and T is an implicit negation or exclusion of the other event, then the ranking should change when the T option is rephrased as follows: "*Linda is a bank teller, whether or not she is active in the feminist movement.*" Tversky and Kahneman have also tried this variant, with no appreciable change in the results. Furthermore, it makes no sense that the linguistic effect of an implicit exclusion should be felt in one of the two cases (in the case of J for Bill and T for Linda), that is, the one that is placed lower in the scale of subjective probabilities, but not in the other, the one that is placed higher. That would be strange indeed. In fact, it will be noted that the list we have just encountered, which was one of the several variants offered to many subjects, puts the conjunction (options A & J, and T & F) *last*, so as not to create spurious linguistic implications. At any rate, this is not necessary and not even important, as many other variants have been tried with very similar results. Even *just* presenting the three options, with no other additional option, preserves the conjunction effect. Therefore, "linguistic" and other objections notwithstanding, the conjunction effect is quite robust. It is indeed a genuine and scary finding about a natural propensity of our mind to violate an elementary probabilistic law, and feel at peace about that. This finding is so disturbing that some psychologists feel compelled to deny it, or at least try to scale it down to utter insignificance.

Another objection to this thesis, recently put forward by the German psychologist Gerd Gigerenzer, argues than this conjunction would *only* show up when we have to decide on a *single* option (for instance, in the case of Bill or that of Linda). Gigerenzer argues that the very idea of probability is inapplicable when we deal with a single instance. The data collected by Gigerenzer and his colleagues refer to judgments such as those made above, but now applied to the probability that our little profiles apply to a hundred bank tellers, a hundred feminist bank tellers, a hundred amateurs of jazz, and so on. They are probabilistic judgments on "collectives," not single individuals such as Bill and Linda. Their findings confirm what Tversky and Kahneman, and others, had already observed in similar experiments: that the conjunction effect does indeed abate considerably, but does not disappear, even when we have to judge the probability for entire groups (the figures are 20–30 percent, no more, *but no less*). It is, however, overwhelming (in the order of 80 percent and above) when we have to determine the likelihood that a single individual exercises this or that profession, or has this or that characteristic.

Gigerenzer has attacked Tversky and Kahneman with studies based on considerations of this sort. He stresses that there are various interpretations of probability and that according to the frequency interpretation, the very idea of probability is inapplicable to single events. Therefore one simply cannot label the conjunction effect as a "fallacy." Gigerenzer does not "side" with any one of these interpretations of probability, wishing to consider them all on an equal footing, but he refuses to see any sign of "irrationality" in our intuitions about typicality and probability.

I note this critique for the sake of completeness, but I do not dwell on it here. (It is treated more fully in Appendix B.) The truth is that there are well-founded counter-objections to Gigerenzer and his collaborators. In essence, it seems perfectly reasonable to all of us to make a judgment as to the probability that a single individual exercises a given profession, indulges in a particular hobby, or is active in one way or another. If, as Gigerenzer argues and as certain other probability theorists have held in the past, it made no sense to guess the probability of a *single* event, then this illusion would be the most *macroscopic* and *interesting* of all our cognitive illusions. For to us ordinary mortals it seems right that to guess the probability of a single event out of several should make sense. Not only that, but we also are prepared to state *which* probability comes closest to our own estimate, and to bet good money on the likelihood that a single event will turn out to be true.

Is this really an illusion? There is both a strictly "frequentist" conception of probability—advanced in the past, for instance, by researchers such as Richard von Mises, Ronald A. Fisher, Jerzy Neiman, and others—and a "subjectivist" idea of probability—advanced, no less convincingly, by those such as Bruno de Finetti and Leonard James Savage. Subjectivists are inclined to give full-blown mathematical rigor to the notion of *the* probability of a *single* event. Here we are talking about truly "abstruse" and complex matters that bear on the very foundation of statistics. I will put them aside before boring the reader too much. In substance, however, it has yet to be demonstrated that "it makes no sense" to talk of the probability of a single event. All of us intuitively believe that to do so does make sense, and a number of major theoreticians confirm that it does. To be subject to cognitive illusions as to *how* we might evaluate such probabilities is one matter, but to deny the very validity of *any* estimate of such single-case probabilities, as Gigerenzer and a few others do, is another matter altogether. As Eldar Shafir has forcefully pointed out to me in conversation, it is a knock-down argument against Gigerenzer's critiques that many events *are* unique, yet we want, and sometimes need, to estimate their likelihood. It would be bizarre (to say the least) to estimate how many Arafats out of 100 would sign a peace treaty with Israel. It is perfectly legitimate in principle, though (as we have seen) difficult in practice, to calculate what exactly the probabilities of such unique events are. (We come back to these points in Appendix B.) The value of the discoveries made by Tversky, Kahneman, and many others stands up against this objection, and many others that precede it.

The conjunction effect has been a target for a great number of criticisms, perhaps because some people are greatly distressed that our species is so irrational. But many experiments of the Bill and Linda type show that this irrationality exists. We would be better off recognizing this fact rather than seeking to refute, or radically interpret, the evidence. I make this rather "technical" aside to show the true value of this discovery.

I might add that the previous objection, the one based on "a play with words," comes up spontaneously in many of our minds, and cannot be passed over in silence. This is not the place in which to refute that objection in detail. What is important is to know that it doesn't work, that there is vastly more at stake here than a mere play with words, and that it is far more important for us to find the real roots of the conjunction effect, wherever these might be—not in traps implicit in language (a hopeless task), but in quite other sorts of psychological traps: in those by-now familiar and omnipresent "typicality" effects (see Chapter 7 and Chapter 9).

At the root of this conjunction effect is a bias: We consider more probable that which we find easier to imagine, that which seems more *typical* to us. Given the profiles of Bill and Linda, it is easier to imagine them, respectively, as accountant and jazz fan, and as bank teller and feminist than it is to imagine them being just *one* of those things and to have no hypothesis about the other. Only thus do we take advantage of at least *some* data in the profile—or so we think. To imagine Bill as an accountant takes advantage of *much* of the information contained in his profile (e.g., his lack of imagination, his skills in mathematics, his lifelessness), just as thinking of Linda as a feminist also uses much of the information offered about her (e.g., her degree in philosophy, her interest in cases of discrimination, her taking part in demonstrations).

So true is this that the accountant in Bill and the feminist in Linda dominate every other characteristic in our intuitive hierarchy of probabilities. Nothing in Bill's profile refers to jazz, and there is nothing in Linda's about banking. Further, some elements in the profile would seem to run against the idea of Bill being interested in jazz, and the same is true about banking for Linda. Both these characteristics seem to us as though they'd been pulled out of a hat, by magic. Any connection between the profiles given and these activities seem to us at best indirect, implausible, and even contraindicated. Bill as jazz fan and Linda as bank teller seem "untypical" to us in the light of what we know from the profile. *And when judgments about what is "typical" come into play, even when they're based on the slightest of evidence, we completely lose sight of any objective probability.* That is why, when we rank only those activities, we rank jazz for Bill and banking for Linda at the bottom of our lists. We really pay no attention to the objective (i.e., demographic, statistically based probabilities about their professions or hobbies) likelihood of either being possible.

Playing jazz for a hobby, or being a bank teller, are properties that apply to many people, and each should in fact lead us to assign it a high probability. But that apart, that Bill plays jazz for a hobby should be far more probable than that *two* properties or activities, two professions or attributes, should be simultaneously engaged in by one person. But this doesn't matter to us. The two conjunctions take advantage of at least *some* of the information provided in the profile, and offer us *some* criteria that we consider "typical." That is why, in spite of even the simplest calculation as to probability, we prefer them. This is, therefore, not an effect of language, nor is it (*pace* Gigerenzer) an anomaly deriving from applying the concept of probability to a single instance, but a clear and symptomatic manifestation of the psychological effect of what we consider typical.

The conjunction effect exists. It is nearly universal, and it should worry us, precisely because, being closely linked to our spontaneous mental processes in regard to what is typical and what isn't, it leads to another mental blind spot, just as widespread and no less troubling: our neglect of base rates. Let's have a look at these.

Tunnel 4: Not Touching Base Rates

As we've just seen, without realizing it, we attach importance to superficial impressions, vague indiscretions, and wishy-washy little biographical summaries. Bill's and Linda's dossiers offer, in fact, little more than vague and generic information, the sort of indiscretions a colleague or a college chum might have dropped about them. Of course, we could say that's all the information we have; and wanting anything more substantial, we should base ourselves on what we know, however vague it is.

But that, too, is not quite the case. The traps set by the "typical" and our prejudices *also work when we know more*. The trouble lies with the fact that though we ought to, we do not actually mobilize all the *pertinent* information we could bring to bear. The perilous cognitive illusions we have already examined (typicality, framing, anchoring, and segregating) are often allied among themselves and then combine with yet another very widespread, insidious, and alarming bias. Let's now take a look at a few examples that have become classics of modern cognitive science.

> Steve is very shy and withdrawn, invariably helpful, but with little interest in people or in the world of reality. A meek and tidy soul, he has a need for order and structure, and a passion for detail.

The objective, once more, is to make a stab at guessing what kind of work Steve might do. Given a list of professions and occupations, we are asked to list them in decreasing order of likelihood. Included among them are farmer and librarian. You can rest assured that these are not in any way coupled or combined. Each job is listed singly—no fear, in this case, of any conjunction trap.

Which is more probable: that Steve is a farmer or that he is a librarian? Given what we have been told about him, there is little doubt that librarian will win out over farmer. If we had to bet on it, we would choose the library, not the fields.

We should already have sniffed out that once again we are up against typicality, or stereotyping. What we know about Steve is much closer to the image we have of librarians than of farmers. Therefore, *in the absence of further information,* we base ourselves on intuition, on typicality. Are we right to do so?

The heart of the matter here is that it is *untrue to say that we lack further information.* Clearly we have some notion of the demographic relationship between librarians and farmers. How many farmers are there for every librarian? We may not know exactly, but we know that there are more farmers than librarians. In fact, if we think about it, there are *a great many more*—just as a guess, at least 100 times as many. Were we compelled to bet on the matter, would it not be preferable—considering how *little* we know about Steve—to bet on objective demographics rather than on stereotyping? It is at least 100 times more probable that Steve is a farmer than a librarian. This alone should govern our choice, rather than his being shy and withdrawn, being methodical, or having a passion for detail. Can a farmer not be methodical to the point of obsessionality? Might he not be shy, or like order and method? Might he not, in fact, possess all these characteristics? Why, therefore, do we not take into consideration the objective probabilities (which we do not know for certain, but which are clear enough) of there being vastly more farmers than librarians?

The fact is *none* of us do. Though some part of our mind tells us there are rather more farmers than librarians, we seem to have no intention whatever of *using* this information. We take the question out of its probabilistic context, tend to give excessive credence to stereotypical judgments (or rather to clichés about farmers and librarians), and make crass mistakes—mistakes that are contrary to the very information we already have!

This blind spot of ours has some quite clear connotations that are known as the "neglect of base rates." We shall shortly examine some variations on these, but another kind of test can already give us an accurate demonstration of how this neglect works and how powerfully it works psychologically.

Our subject is given a long list of profiles of this sort (including a number of thumbnail sketches quite like Steve's):

> Smith likes to work with precision. He draws and calculates with ease and did well at school in mathematics.
>
> Jones has uncommon communication gifts. He is a fine speaker and knows how to obtain agreement from his audience. At school he did well in classics and history.

The subject is given a list of such abbreviated dossiers (of which the above two are a sample) and is told that these dossiers (note with care) contain, in no particular order, 70 percent engineers and 30 percent lawyers. The purpose is to guess which are (presumably) engineers and which are lawyers, and then to subdivide them by category into two separate lists.

Having just studied Steve's case, we can readily imagine what happens: Smith will be identified as an engineer and Jones as a lawyer. We pay no heed to the fact that an engineer may have outstanding communications skills or that a lawyer might perfectly well have been good at mathematics. Our stereotyping capacity (that of our mental clichés) will take over.

But the crucial discovery we make with this test is something else again, and the results show that, *even when the subject is told that the list contains 70 lawyers and 30 engineers*, the profiles are, to all intents and purposes, split into two parts in almost exactly the same way—even when the two percentages are *explicitly* inverted! In other words, though we are now told that there are 7 lawyers for every 3 engineers, this means very little to us. We put our profiles into two categories almost entirely on the basis of what is "typical." We trust our mental clichés even when we have *additional information.* The most elementary and basic demographic information we set almost completely aside. This, in its most basic form, is what we mean by the *neglect of base rates.* This neglect is not total and unshakable, but is still large enough and resilient enough to be a serious cause for worry.

It is worth stressing that we all tend to use these base rates—that is, the available information (such as the explicitly stated percentages of engineers versus lawyers)—correctly, when we have no other information. By which I mean, no other information at all. In the absence of *any* personality profile of the kind we have just seen, we do go by the percentages. But when a profile appears, however uninformative it may be, we neglect the base rates. Imagine that after being told that our sample contains 70 lawyers and 30 engineers, we have to decide whether the following individual—let's call him Dick— is a lawyer or an engineer.

> Dick is a 30-year-old man. He is married with no children.
> A man of high ability and high motivation, he promises to be
> quite successful in his field. He is well liked by his colleagues.

This skimpy profile is artfully designed to convey no infor- mation relevant to the question of whether Dick is a lawyer or an engineer. Consequently, the stated proportions of lawyers to engineers, and these alone, should govern our speculation. One would think that a totally uninformative profile would be treated as having exactly as much value, or as little value, as no profile at all. Yet this isn't the case. In fact, most of us disregard the stated proportions and judge the probability of Dick being a lawyer as about 50/50, as though we were tossing a coin. Worthless evidence is not regarded, as it should be, as being the same as no evidence at all. It is a psychological fact that when we are offered worthless evidence we ignore prior proba- bilities, but when we are offered no evidence at all, then prior probabilities are correctly taken into account. These are some of the complex and disturbing characteristics of the mental tunnel called neglect of base rates.

It would be a mistake not to recognize how persuasively and how *unconsciously* this illusion works on us to produce *incorrigible* prejudices about certain groups of human beings, individuals, and cultures. Racism draws its strength from many other sources, but this is certainly one of them. Our failure to take account of the real base rates is independent of ideologies and political doctrine—in short, it is something that happens to us regardless of what we actually *think*. This cognitive error is one of the most insidious. We will return to these often unconscious and diabolical mental blind spots.

Tunnel 5: Misplaced Causality

A certain town is served by two hospitals. In the larger hospital about 45 babies are born each day, and in the smaller hospital about 15 babies are born each day. As you know, about 50 percent of all babies are boys. The exact percentage of baby boys, however, varies from day to day. Sometimes it may be higher than 50 percent, sometimes lower.

For a period of one year, each hospital recorded the days on which (more/less) than 60 percent of the babies born were boys. Which hospital do you think recorded more such days?

Before you make your choice, a brief note. Obviously, the usual pattern is for births to average roughly 50 percent for each sex. Equally obvious is that the percentage will not be exactly 50 percent every day. There will be days when one sex or another (it doesn't matter which) will predominate. The special days, those that are duly registered, are those on which the balance is disproportionate, to 60 percent or more of one sex.

I recommend that before continuing, the reader think carefully and provide his or her own justification for that reply. (The average response obtained by Tversky, Kahneman, and

Bar-Hillel in a series of noted experiments, known as "The Maternity Ward," are to be found in "Tunnel Exits.")

Have you reflected? Good. Whatever reply you made, we are now (as the Israeli psychologist Maya Bar-Hillel did) about to make a minor change to the data. Let us now suppose that in each clinic we henceforth also note the days in which *all* the births are of the same sex. Which of the two clinics will register a greater number of such days? Again, think!

At this very point, if we take the average of all answers given in the past to this particular test, more than half of us should begin to be aware of a certain perplexity. I am not yet ready to say what is involved, and why; it is enough to note that on the basis of these two successive queries, and those *alone,* many of us (in fact, the majority) understand that something has gone wrong with our reasoning. Can it be that what holds good for the "more than 60 percent" is completely changed when we talk about 100 percent of births of the same sex? What would we say if the births were 80 percent of the same sex? Our heads now begin to sort matters out; we reconsider our initial judgment, and may begin to catch a glimpse of the right reply.

A powerful intuition is at work in many of us, and it merits being made explicit and discussed: We perceive that, biologically, the sex of each birth is obviously not dependent on the hospital in which a child is born; therefore . . . .

The first part of this intuition is entirely correct, but the conclusion we draw from it is a crass mistake, a genuine illusion. The biological mechanism that determines the sex of each child is as we know it, and it does indeed show that the probable gender of each child hovers very close to 50 percent for every birth. It is *true* that we start with a biological mechanism that produces an average of 50 percent, but we are talking here about a *statistical fluctuation.* In solving our problem, it is *irrelevant* that the choice of hospital has nothing to do with determining the sex of the children born there. A well-established fluctuation (deviating in this case up to 10 percent from the average) is the more likely to occur, the *smaller* the sample.

We should not confuse the *cause* (in this case, biological) of a particular phenomenon with the probability of a casual fluctuation in the *consequences* thereof. These are two distinct worlds and this we generally do not see. We find it hard to make that distinction; therein lies one of our widespread cognitive illusions. Here is how we can state this even more clearly:

> If a mother's eyes are blue, what is the probability of her daughter having blue eyes?
> What is the probability of a mother having blue eyes, if her daughter's eyes are blue?

Repeated tests show that most of us assign a higher probability to the first than the second. But this is a mistake. A statistical correlation should be a two-way affair; it should be symmetrical. The "diagnostic value" of estimating the probability of a mother and daughter having blue eyes is absolutely the same whether one starts with the mother's blue eyes or the daughter's. The laws of genetics make this perfectly symmetrical calculation of probability true. The color of a mother's eyes is, via the well-known mechanisms of genetics, a clue for a causal link with the color of her daughter's eyes, but the color of her daughter's eyes cannot in any sense be a clue of a causal factor affecting the color of her mother's eyes. This is also true, but totally irrelevant. *Objective correlations of frequency do not reflect this asymmetrical relationship between cause and effect.*

We do not like to take this into account. A common cause is generally held to be more "diagnostic" of its effect (i.e., more likely to indicate its presence) than the common effect is of its cause. We refuse to admit that the reverse side of the coin—that which goes from effect back to probable cause—is equally compelling in statistical correlation, or "diagnosis." This is, as the "maternity ward" test (in which the gender of babies is not related to the number born in a given maternity ward) shows, a totally characteristic cognitive illusion.

If we combine this illusion with "typicality" and "framing," we can easily see what happens in the classic Ralph and Jane case. Jane complains that Ralph is forever stepping on her feet when they dance; Ralph says he is an experienced dancer and does no such thing. How do we verify which of them is telling the truth? Well, one way is obvious. We can see whether Ralph steps on the feet of other dancing partners. Few of us, however, find it as obvious to see whether other dancers also step on Jane's feet, and only on her feet! If that were so, then Ralph would be innocent, and Jane would be the dancer who's always out of step.

But here, the framing effect makes us see only Ralph as the clumsy dancer and Jane as the victim. The asymmetric diagnosis error, which favors cause over effect, builds on that. Add typicality and the job is done, for men are clumsy and women twinkle-toed! Poor Ralph! Poor we, who are all victims of similar blind spots!

Tunnel 6: To the Bitter End

The maternity ward problem may have given us some amusement; it probably didn't seem especially alarming. In real life, after all, such problems do not arise. The same is true of Ralph and Jane; it could seem a kind of joke. The time has come to look at these very same cognitive illusions in realistic terms and in more dramatic circumstances, such as might well worry us.

By now the reader is on guard against certain kinds of cognitive illusions, but just by changing a few of the basic data we are likely to fall back into the same errors and fall prey again to them.

Here is a first problem, known as the clinical test.

A clinical test, designed to diagnose a specific illness, comes out positive for a certain patient.
We are told that:

1. The test is 79 percent reliable (that is, it gives a false positive rate of 21 percent);

2. On average, this illness affects 1 percent of the population in the same age group as the patient.

Taking this into account, and assuming you know nothing
about the patient's symptoms or signs, what is the probability
that this patient actually has the illness?

Some of us may have recognized in this test a kind of reasoning seen in the last problem: a form of sophism that makes
us confuse cause with probability. We start with a correct, a very
correct, intuition and draw an erroneous conclusion. The way
our minds work, we are likely to think that part 2 has been
added just to confuse us. After all, what does the average rate
of incidence have to do with anything, once the test has been
given and the result is positive? Does the reliability of the test
depend on the average incidence of this particular illness in
the population as a whole—that is, on independent data calculated before our patient submitted to the test? Of course not!
The reliability of a clinical test is something related only to
itself; it does not depend on demographic data. Reliability is a
matter of biochemical purity, of cells, molecules, instruments;
it is not linked to population averages. Many people reason
this way, and they answer with some confidence that the probability of our patient being infected is 79 percent.

There are others who give a certain credence to part 2,
who rightly intuit that the reliability of the test, though determined by purity, molecules, and the rest, must be *combined* with
a base-rate probability based on the population as a whole to
determine whether an individual patient is affected. But even
these—as many tests given to U.S. hospital doctors show—still
think that, in light of the positive test, the probability for
Patient X is more than 50 percent. Given the test result, a vast
majority think it more likely the patient has the illness than
not.

The statistically correct answer, which can be established
by Bayes' law (see Chapter 5) is 8 percent. That's right, 8 percent!

It sounds crazy. Most of us, on being told the real probability, take refuge in one of three reactions: The result is wrong
(we've made some error in calculation); Bayes' law, whatever
that is, is not applicable to such cases; or *if that's the probability,
it's not even worth having the test!* Come on! The test is highly reliable (79 percent is not peanuts), the patient tests positive, and
still his chances of being infected are only 8 percent?
Something's wrong here.

Something is indeed wrong. But it isn't the test, nor Bayes'
law. What doesn't work is our intuition when dealing with risk
and probability. We'll come back shortly to the whys and
wherefores of this, but one thing should strike us right away:
Why are we left unmoved by the fact that, thanks to the test,
the probability of Patient X having the disease is eight times
greater? What use, after all, is a test? (The explanation for this
calculation is in "Tunnel Exits.") And isn't it crazy on our part
to consider a 1 percent probability "just about the same" as an
8 percent? We'll come back to these points and show how
Bayes' law is exactly what is rationally and scientifically needed
for these cases.

Of course one can say, well, we don't even know what this
Bayes' law is! So how can we come up with a correct answer if
we don't know the right way to arrive at it? Suppose we didn't
even know such a formula for calculating probability existed?

The truth is, no one asked us to calculate it *exactly*. Frankly,
it would have been a lot better if we'd had the guts sincerely
(and not just through mental sloth) to say we had not the faint-
est idea what the probability was. Or if we'd said 10 or even 20
percent. That would have given us no cause for alarm. There
would have been no question of a cognitive illusion or a mental blind spot. The trouble lies in the fact that our guesswork
was so wildly wrong, and that *we think we know how to come up
with an answer.* We believe this so strongly that we are shocked
and incredulous when we are told the right answer. Even those
who don't think the probability is 79 percent come up with fig-

ures far closer to 60 percent than to 8 percent. We are wrong by a factor of 7, or even more!

Our failure to pay attention to base rates and our confusion of causes with diagnostic correlations (and here the term *diagnostic* truly comes into its own!) here join together and, all unknown to us, exert a malevolent force.

Equally alarming is the following case, in which we shift from hospitals to a court of law. The instance is no less dramatic, and the consequences are every bit as destructive.

Here is the so-called juror's fallacy. We should try to imagine it as perfectly real, for any one of us could be called onto a jury to decide a similar case.

> You are a member of a jury. A taxi driver is accused of having run down a pedestrian on a stormy night and having fled the scene of the accident. The prosecutor, in asking for a conviction, bases his whole case on a single witness, a lady who saw the accident from her window a little way away. The lady testifies that she saw the pedestrian struck by a blue taxi and then saw that taxi drive away from the scene of the accident. The accused works for a taxi company whose taxis are all blue. During the trial, the following emerges:
>
> 1. There are only two taxi companies in this town. The whole fleet of one company is green; the other has only blue cabs. Eighty-five percent of all the taxis on the road that night were green, and only 15 percent were blue.
>
> 2. The single witness has undergone a number of vision tests in conditions similar to those of the night of the accident. She has been shown to be able to distinguish a blue taxi from a green one 80 percent of the time.
>
> On the basis of the sworn testimony of the witness, and the data offered in 1 and 2, what is the probability that the taxi really was blue?

What say you, the jury?

Our spontaneous reaction is going to be exactly as in the clinical test. The lady's eyesight is not dependent on the number of green and blue taxis on the street that night. That is quite right. We then conclude that if her eyesight is 80 percent correct, the probability of the taxi being blue is also 80 percent. That may seem a little high, yet the majority of the subjects tested by Tversky and Kahneman nonetheless consider the probability of the taxi being blue higher than 50 percent. That is, they consider it more likely that the taxi was blue than green.

We are now aware enough to suspect that our intuitive reasoning here might be governed by a cognitive illusion, and so it is. Once again, we should have combined the reliability of the witness with the a priori probability of her having seen, in perfectly good faith, what she claims she saw. We have to take into account the base frequency of the number of cabs on the road. The correct answer, the one a responsible juror should have come up with, is 41 percent (see the calculation in "Tunnel Exits"). Bayes' law, in short, tells us that it is significantly *less* likely that the cab was blue. Had there been no witness to the accident at all, the probability would have been only 15 percent, as in 1. With the witness, the probability rises to 41 percent, but not higher. This may seem paradoxical or implausible. But that is due to our blind spot: We disregard base frequencies and we confuse cause and diagnostic correlation.

The great empiricist philosopher David Hume had sufficient insight to suggest "a general maxim worthy of our attention." That maxim says, "No testimony is sufficient to establish a miracle unless the testimony be of such a kind that its falsehood would be more miraculous than the fact which it endeavors to establish." As we have seen, a witness can easily give false testimony in perfectly good faith. Between good faith and reliable testimony lie the heuristics and the blinds spots we have been discussing. The cognitive illusions shown up by this blind spot are so universal and so pertinacious that we would be wise enough (and lucky enough) to remain in good health and never find ourselves wrongly accused of a crime we did not commit.

Tunnel 7: The Certainty Effect

Imagine yourself in the situations described below, and think sincerely what you might do.

SITUATION 1

When we went to the movies last week, we were inadvertently exposed to a rare and fatal virus. The possibility of actually contracting the disease is 1 in 1,000, but once you have the illness there is no known cure. On the other hand, we can readily, and now, be given an injection that stops the development of the illness. Unfortunately, these injections are only available in very small quantities and are sold to the highest bidder. What is the highest price you would be prepared to pay for such an injection?

Having thought it out carefully, note your highest bid on a piece of paper. Now consider the following situation.

SITUATION 2

This one is identical to the previous situation, with the following modifications:

The probability of catching the illness is now 4 in 1,000. The injection works in only 25 percent of the cases, which reduces the risk to 3 in 1,000. In this case, what is the maximum you would offer?

Again, note your maximum bid. Now consider the following.

SITUATION 3

A group of research scientists in the School of Medicine are running laboratory experiments on this particular virus. They are seeking volunteers to participate in a set of trials. The subjects are asked to take a risk of infection amounting to 1 in 1,000, but to do so voluntarily (whereas in the previous two cases they had been infected involuntarily). In this case, the injections will never be available to the general public, and the risk of death remains at 1 in 1,000. The 20 volunteers who submit the lowest bids (whatever these are) will be chosen. What is the lowest bid you would submit to accept to take part in this experiment?

After you have noted your three bids, you can compare the results with the average bids made by a number of people who took part in this test (see "Tunnel Exits").

The certainty effect also leads to a variety of subtle and interesting results that I drastically simplify by offering the following imaginary case:

> We have inherited a luxurious house in California, and we have decided not to sell it. We decide to insure it against earthquakes. Normal earthquake insurance costs $600 a year for every $1 million of property insurance. One of the major insurance companies auctions off a limited number of policies at a reduced rate. These special policies contain a clause that makes them valid only on Tuesdays, Thursdays, and Saturdays.
> What is the highest sealed bid you will submit for this partial risk coverage?

So as not to deprive the reader of the pleasure in replying honestly, I suggest a brief pause. You should not go on reading until you have made up your mind.

The certainty effect consists in seeking a greater financial recompense for accepting a low risk of death than we would be willing to pay to eliminate an equivalent risk to which, through no fault of our own, we have *already* been exposed. Further, as the results show, and as the reader can readily verify from her own answers, the *total* elimination of a 1 in 1,000 risk is worth at least three times a "simple" reduction of *the same* risk by an amount of *exactly* 1 in 1,000. The fact that these reactions of ours seem to us "obvious" and "natural" just shows how complete our blind spot is, and how strongly we feel the certainty effect.

Rationally and objectively, the three bids we make should be identical. Obviously, no abstract calculation can tell us *how much* we should bid on our own lives. But it does tell us that that sum, whatever it is, should be equal in all three situations.

In the imaginary and highly simplified insurance case, one would arrive at a rational price for the "special" policy by multiplying the full price ($600) by the amount of coverage offered, three-sevenths of the full price, or $257. As similar, though much more refined, tests with a variety of subjects show, however, the average offer turns out to be significantly lower than the theoretically calculated "fair price." In the somewhat crude case I just presented, many, in fact, would probably claim not to be at all interested in such a policy. The certainty effect is in full play here. Full coverage against any risk is worth far more than a "simple" reduction of risk. But a policy at, say, $120 a year should be *highly* attractive. That is a reduction of four-fifths, or 80 percent, and it would guarantee coverage of three-sevenths of the risk, a coverage of 43 percent. But the feeling of "certainty" we obtain from the "full" policy is a total illusion. If the insurance business had any "certainties" whatsoever, no insurance policy would ever be offered. The only element in an insurance policy that is fully known is the amount of the annual premium. The rest is all a question of probability. If we "don't care" about such calculations, and demand "certainty," then we are well and truly prisoners of our blind spots and have no intention of setting them aside, however briefly.

If you add to this the regret factor, then a sensible man would seek to cover one blind spot with another. Many people are stuck with the thought, "But supposing there really is an earthquake on one of the days for which I'm not covered. What would I say to my wife and children? How could I forgive myself for having taken up a reduced policy?" We've already

seen how heavily this regret factor may weigh (see Chapter 1).
Avoiding causes of future regret is certainly not always irrational. If I know that the urge to smoke will become overwhelming later in the day, and that I will deeply regret my having
indulged in the habit, it may be a good idea to preemptively
throw the pack into the trash. It may be irrational, under certain circumstances, *not* to avoid causes of future and justified
regret. The Harvard philosopher Thomas Shelling has amply
and insightfully studied these splits in our decision making. It
is as though there were one "decisor" that is prone to indulge,
and a different and better "decisor" that takes preliminary precautions now against the "takeover" by this other, "lower"
decisor later on. They both dwell within one and the same person, and their fights, covenants, and truces are a constant
source of subjective psychological tension, and of interesting
objective philosophical problems. This is, once more, a sub-
domain of the theory of rationality that imposes very subtle distinctions and very thorough analyses. However, its importance
is purely psychological; very often it has no basis in rationality.
If, and I emphasize the word *if,* we were rationally convinced
that we'd made the best possible economic choice when we
bought our policy, then we *shouldn't* feel any regret. If the
quake strikes on one of the uncovered days, we will certainly be
unhappy, but we shouldn't be devoured by regret. The "justification" offered by regret explains one cognitive illusion by
introducing another, and this explanation, in some cases at
least, may become totally irrational.

The less the reader is convinced by the correctness and
rationality of these considerations and these "abstruse" calculations, the happier I am. The certainty effect is one of the deep-
est and most dangerous blind spots we know. Its manifestations
in the economy, in politics, in military strategy, in insurance,
and in our daily lives are innumerable. Now that we have
learned to recognize them, the reader is invited to discover
countless other examples in the world about us. Through
thinking enough about these matters, one day we may come to
a certain rationality. Unless, that is, the students of MIT are

right with their joke that, "A light at the end of the tunnel can only be the light on a train coming in the opposite direction!" Their joke is the opposite of ours. They, poor devils, are subjected to a constant overdose of rationality.

Tunnel 8: The Uncertainty Effect, or Irrational Prudence

The proverb says that one can never be too prudent. But decision theorists are not of that opinion. Indeed, at the beginning of the 1950s, a prominent U.S. probabilist, Leonard James Savage, formulated a universal principle about rational decisions that he called the "sure-thing principle." This is, in substance, his argument: If, after considering all the arguments pro and con, we decide to do something and a certain condition arises in that something, *and* we decide to do *that very thing*, even if the condition does *not* arise, then, according to the Savage principle, we should act immediately, *without waiting*. If we wait, we may not be able, as the reader will soon see, to do what we planned to do at all.

This sure-thing principle should, at least when we view it dispassionately, abstractly, and in the light of reason, seem incontestable to us. But once again, between saying and doing, between knowing this with our minds and deciding to do it with our intuition, a blind spot occurs. Our species has maintained this tunnel within, like all the other comparable tunnels, from the beginning of time, but it was identified and methodically explored by cognitive scientists only in 1992. We now begin to explore it approximately and at large, starting with one of its most intuitive, though not very precise, points of entry.

For instance, if my appointment with one of my most important clients is confirmed, I will go to New York City tomorrow. My client perhaps can't be reached until tomorrow, but as I think about it, I realize there are a number of other things I could profitably do in New York to get things moving, and it might be that knowing that I'm in New York, my client will be more likely to see me. So, all things considered, even if I don't get my appointment, it would be a good idea to go anyway. Shouldn't I then make a reservation on the plane *right away*, even before my appointment is confirmed?

This simplistic approach of the Savage principle may seem fairly obvious. But let me change the example somewhat. Suppose there is no way to know, before tomorrow, whether that client can see me. Suppose, too, that I have other reasons—these are equally valid but *completely* different from the reasons expressed above—to go to New York tomorrow, and not some other day (e.g., tickets for a show, a date with an old flame, a visit to a sick uncle whom I like). Suppose, finally, that my business appointment, confirmed at the very last moment (for instance, when I am already in New York), will certainly make it impossible for me to do any of the other things I want to do.

Here is one of the ways into the tunnel, and at the same time a mild disavowal of the sure-thing principle. Ask yourself, honestly, whether in these circumstances you would book your plane *now*, and whether you would take off to New York in the morning, not sure at all whether this trip of yours is *then* going to be a business trip or a trip you undertake only for personal reasons. In this hypothetical (but pretty realistic) case, it is certain that *one* of the two reasons for your trip will be satisfied, but not both. Furthermore, both when you reserve your seat and when you later leave, you have no way of knowing *which* of your two reasons for going will be satisfied. You won't know that until you reach New York.

We can confidently wager that most of us, given this scenario, would decide to *postpone* the trip to New York, even though tomorrow seems a particularly suitable day. We would think that we lacked "sufficient" reason to book our ticket and fly. Yes, there are two different orders of motives, each perfectly valid, and such that (given the circumstances) one of the two will certainly be satisfied; but *first* we all want to know *which*. The either/or alternative, known in the language of logic as a "disjunction," which in this case should be sufficient to bring us to act, turns out to be insufficient. Reserving our flight, taking off from the airport, feeling uncertain, we would feel we were acting without a proper "because."

Not particularly rationally—and violating, at least in certain respects, the Savage principle—we *fail* to make certain decisions, so much so that if someone else points out to us the peculiarity of our non–decision making, we are often led to rise from our torpor and resolve to act. Just by laying out for their subjects all the moves of the game and their likely consequences, Amos Tversky and Eldar Shafir discovered this decision-making "reawakening" phenomenon. Strange as it may seem, when we face two or more situations and don't know which will unfold in the future, though knowing that one of them will certainly happen, our imagination gets totally blocked. Taking one at a time, we know perfectly well how to calculate the consequences of each of these possible scenarios, but we are not thereby led to consider the consequences of their disjunction, to imagine *now* what we would do if one or the other eventuality, but we do not know which one, turned out true.

Before we know with certainty which among these eventualities will actually happen, our will and our power to make decisions remain paralyzed. In many situations of *true* uncertainty, this is the wise and prudent course; not to do something may be entirely rational. But here it is not rational, for we have *all* the elements necessary to conclude that we will make the *same* decision whichever eventuality comes about. At that point we enter the tunnel of disjunction; we are held up by an excessive and irrational prudence. In fact, as Tversky and Shafir have shown in perfectly rigorous, and therefore more elaborate, cases, often all that is necessary is that the subject be shown the paradox of his behavior for him to decide to act.

In the case of the trip to New York, this is what we might say to our interlocutor: "Look, if the appointment is confirmed, then you say you will certainly fly to New York. If the appointment doesn't turn out, you tell me you will go to New York anyway—for other, personal reasons. You don't know, and you won't know until tomorrow, whether you will be able to see your client. Therefore, you say, you want to wait. But are you sure you really do want to put off your trip? Are you sure this "therefore" holds up? Think again. Look, you wouldn't hesitate to make a reservation and take the trip if you knew for sure that you were going on a business trip. Nor would you hesitate to do both if you were sure that you were going to New York for personal reasons. Right? But one or the other of the two reasons is *sure* to work out. The only logical "therefore," then, is to act *anyway* and book your seat."

At this point your subject may begin to think; he may rise up from his decision-making doldrums. It remains for us to give him a little push: "I know you don't feel like making a reservation and traveling to New York. First you need to know, *now*, for which of the two reasons, both of them strongly motivating, you claim to be going to New York. But, you see, both of them require the same decision; each pushes you to make the same move: a reservation, a flight. Therefore, you ought to act promptly. If you hesitate, if you temporize, you're putting both at risk: the appointment with your client and the other things you want to do."

With this sort of urging therapy, based on the simple logic of decision making, and the sure-thing principle, you can make someone else realize that his prudence may well be excessive, even irrational. For this prudence of ours—which is normal, most natural, indeed, nearly irresistible—must sometimes be overruled; one needs to learn to act, to decide, to get out of the disjunctive, either/or tunnel and rid ourselves of this irrational prudence.

Amos Tversky tells the story of how he became aware of this particular blind spot and its power. It happens that two new professorships were open in his department of psychology at Stanford University, and after short-listing many fine candidates Tversky and his colleagues settled on the two they thought the best. The one chosen for the first professorship was, if you will pardon the ungrammaticality of the expression, "more better" than the other. Nonetheless, the candidate for the second chair had also been selected. But Tversky and his colleagues decided *not* to offer the professorship to the second candidate *until* the first had accepted or refused. In fact, as Tversky admits, whatever the first candidate did, whether he accepted or not, the second appointment would have been made. All of them knew that—at least on paper. But all of them decided (Tversky, too, at first) not to make their offer to the second candidate until the first had either accepted or refused the *other* chair. As a psychologist, Tversky thought about the reasons for this unnecessary delay, and realized he had come across a generalized phenomenon deserving of further study, now called the disjunction fallacy. The following are some of the precise tests undertaken since this professional mishap.

SITUATION 1

You've just played roulette, betting $100 on the black. You won. So now you have $200. Are you willing to bet another $100, on either black or red?

It doesn't matter whether you choose black or red. The important thing is, knowing that you've just won, would you bet again, with the same probability (50/50) of winning or losing? You might as easily be betting on heads or tails. Tests show that the majority of people answer yes. The fact that you won makes you bolder; you feel you're now rich enough to have another shot at winning more.

SITUATION 2

You've just bet $100 on the black at roulette, and it lost. Would you bet another $100?

Many say yes. They hope to recoup with another bet.

SITUATION 3

You've just bet $100 on roulette in a neighboring room. The wheel has stopped turning, with the result that either you've won $200 or you've lost your bet. But you don't know yet which. Are you willing to bet another $100 before you know whether you've won or lost? (In the case of a coin, we can imagine the toss as having taken place, but the coin is still concealed.)

Those who would bet again now, before knowing, are a narrow minority. These betting offers, to elicit a clean and indubitable disjunction effect, are presented separately to each subject: the first now, the second a week later, and the third another week down the line. If you add up the responses obtained from those subjects who are willing to bet again in case they have won *and* in case they have lost, then the most frequent systematic pattern is: I would bet again if I know I've lost, and bet again if I know I've won, but I won't bet again if I don't know whether I've won or lost. The disjunction effect strongly influences the responses of this class of subjects, the most interesting one from our point of view. Of course, not everyone will bet again if she wins, nor if she has lost. But among those who say they would bet again when they have won *and* also (separately) say they would bet again when they have lost, a majority would refuse to bet again if they were uncertain as to the result of their previous bet.

There is an elegant demonstration that it is not the *wording* of the problem that explains this effect (it is not the appearance of the disjunctive expressions "either . . . or," or "whether . . . or," as such). In fact, these authors have shown that there is no disjunctive effect at all when the subject wins in both possible situations. In essence, if you are willing to bet again knowing that you've won $100 and you are willing to bet again knowing that you've won $200, then you are *still* willing to bet again when you know that you have won but don't know whether you have won $100 or $200. In this "all win" case, the actual percentage of "willing" subjects in the disjunctive situation is exactly the average of the percentages of willing subjects in each of the nondisjunctive ones. (For obvious reasons, this is exactly the figure that the good theory of decisions prescribes.) Once again, there can be no "linguistic" explanation of these results, based on possible misunderstandings or on a sort of "intrinsic" perplexity that subjects might develop toward certain problem situations simply because these are formulated in a disjunctive "language."

As with all our other blind spots, this prudence in the face of uncertainty seems to us perfectly natural. We have no difficulty in accepting the conclusions of Tversky and Shafir; at heart, we think we would behave in exactly the same way. We recognize ourselves in these responses, revealing the disjunction effect in its purest form.

An analogous experiment by Tversky and Shafir is the following test given to students at Stanford University:

> You've just handed in a difficult exam. You'll know the day after tomorrow whether you passed or failed. You are offered a real bargain in the form of a vacation in Hawaii for less than $200, but you have to decide by tomorrow and hand in a non-reimbursable deposit of $50. You can put off the decision for a day (by which time you will know for sure whether you passed or failed) for an additional $15, which is neither reimbursable nor deducted from the total price of your package. What do you decide to do?
>
> The students were then asked what they would decide if (a) they knew they had passed, (b) they knew they had failed, or (c) they did not know whether they had passed or failed.

The majority of students said they would pay the deposit, which would be included in the final price, if they were sure they'd passed (the vacation being a sort of prize). A slightly greater majority said they would pay the deposit, included in the final price, if they knew they'd failed (here, the vacation is a form of consolation). In either case, however, when they knew the result for sure, and knew whether they'd passed or failed, *very few* were attracted to the idea of laying out an extra $15, in effect money thrown away, just to defer the decision. If uncertain of the result, only a *minority* said they were willing to pay the advance deposit, but for these the nonreturnable, "throwaway" $15 option (which bought no more than a delayed decision) sold like hotcakes. In case of uncertainty, a majority were willing and eager to spent the extra $15 to make sure of their result.

To sum up the responses, the majority buy if they know they've passed, buy if they know they've failed, and do not buy (or take the $15 extra option to await the decision) when they do not know which. As with the roulette problem or tossing a coin, most of us find the reasoning of the Stanford students perfectly sensible; we would act in the same way, and again we would fall victim to an excess of prudence.

There is, of course, an "explanation" (a word I put in quotes because there is nothing at all rational about it). As Tversky and Shafir point out in their analysis of the results, when it is a question of not knowing an outcome, their students have no good "reason" to decide. They don't feel up to booking this bargain trip to Hawaii because when they are called upon to make a reservation they do not know whether they are doing so because they are (a) celebrating passing or (b) consoling themselves for a failure. Again, they fly in the face of the Savage principle: To them, it matters not one whit that the action is *identical* and that there are good reasons for acting immediately and whatever the outcome of their exam. They act instead on a psychological principle of having insufficient reason. To decide or act (in this case, to make a reservation), we seem to require *a* good reason. Two *possible* reasons, equally valid but different, do not "suffice": Even if we know with certainty that tomorrow, when we know the result, one or the other will give us that good reason to go, and that both will lead to an identical result.

I have deliberately simplified this finding in order to urge us all to take it into account in our daily lives and to be constantly on guard against it. However, the disjunction effect, when examined in its proper scientific context, is quite subtle and fragile, and this must also be stressed. I have already alluded to the powerful "therapeutic" procedure of forcing people to "think through" the fact that they will do the same no matter what. When this is properly laid out in the mind's eye, then subjects do not choose to wait. As Eldar Shafir rightly specifies, the disjunction effect basically relies on the tendency *not* to think about the separate branches when facing the disjunction. The cases we have just examined should not be taken as revealing a willful resistance to the logic behind the sure-thing principle. The more introspectively inclined readers might well be skeptical that it may *ever* happen to them to be in the grips of the disjunction effect. In fact, when we *do* see the applicability of the logic of the sure-thing principle to the situation at hand, then we are naturally inclined to act accordingly. The point is that often we do not see its applicability and therefore fall for the disjunction effect, becoming irrationally prudent. We show this below with a slightly more elaborate experiment, based on a situation known to economists and decision theorists as the prisoner's dilemma.

Tversky and Shafir also carried out other experiments in which the subjects had to choose between a strategy of cooperation or of competition with an unknown adversary (in their experiment, an imaginary student, presented as also linked to the university's computer network). These are models well known to the experts, and rather more complicated than we have presented so far. The essence of the matter here shines with full force; the disjunctive effect becomes clear and powerful.

In substance, this experiment involves submitting the subject to a simulated economic game, in which he knows that his adversary has *already* chosen his strategy and that there is *no possibility whatever* that his own decision will *influence* his adversary's. In this dilemma, studied by economists since the end of the 1940s, the following situation always ensues: If both contenders compete, they both find themselves worse off than if they had cooperated. If, however, one of the two competes and the other cooperates, the one who competes finds himself in the best available position, whereas the noncompetitor finds himself in the worst. Game theory has established that when one cannot communicate with an adversary (and therefore cannot seek to cooperate) and has no way to predict the way a competitor is going to decide, it is *always* better to compete with complete selfishness.

This scenario is traditionally known as the prisoner's dilemma, because it can be posed as that of two prisoners, each suspected of a crime, each held in a different cell, and each separately summoned to confess and incriminate the other by a promise of a much reduced sentence. Here, the theory (and that sorry practice of the police at all times and all over the world) holds that one should always confess. An identical dilemma in economics suggests that one should always compete. For a prisoner, in fact, "competing" (with an accomplice) results in confession, and cooperating (with an accomplice) means not confessing. The interesting result is that in Tversky and Shafir's experiments, presented as an interaction in a computer network, a large majority of subjects (67 percent) reach their decision on the following basis: "I choose to compete if I *know* (note the word) my accomplice has decided to compete; I choose to compete if I *know* my accomplice has decided to cooperate; I choose to cooperate if I don't yet *know* what he has done." That last bit should be underlined: not what he will do, but what he has done.

The disjunction effect, as we can see, shows up in all its red-blooded power in models of economic choice. It involves this curious kind of reasoning: "My choice can in no way influence the bottom line, because my adversary's decision has *already* been made. But I don't know what it is, *therefore* I will cooperate." Here's that famous "therefore" again. This decision is not particularly logical or rational, and in these simulated games it is in fact decidedly damaging to our own interests. The "therefore," however, offers us a convenient alibi for the irrationality of our prudence. The "explanation" for this behavior (again, the word is in quotation marks because, though exerting a strong psychological pressure, it, too, is totally irrational) is that we choose to act in the way we *wish* our adversary had acted. As we well know, our choice has no influence on someone else's choice. If we know *what* choice the other has made, then we make the most advantageous choice possible for ourselves. If, on the other hand, though we know our adversary's decision has already been made (and thus we cannot influence it at all), and we don't know what that choice was, then we choose a state of affairs that we would *like to see* be the case. Tversky and Shafir call this decision process "quasi-magical thought." It's the sort of thinking that takes over the man playing dice: He will roll the dice harder if he wants a five or a six and more gently if he's looking for a one or a two. These different rolls have been experimentally demonstrated in due form. The player knows perfectly well that the outcome he wants does not depend on how he rolls the dice, but he can't help trying. His muscles secretly depend on the quasi-magic of his psyche.

It's Not True, but I Believe It: Quasi-Magical Thought

Disjunction is only one of many fascinating tunnels in the world of quasi-magical thought. "It's not true, but I believe it" could be a motto for all of them. A true story illustrates this perfectly. It comes from the life of Niels Bohr, the Danish physicist and Nobel Prize winner and one of the fathers of atomic physics and quantum theory. On his wall hung a horseshoe, and one visitor, astonished to see it hanging on his wall, said, "But Professor Bohr, surely you can't believe in such a stupid superstition!" Bohr answered, "Of course I don't, but they tell me it works even if I don't believe in it!"

Quasi-magical thought, for all its innocence and its precarious balance between the serious and the facetious, raises problems. It breaks the link that should solidly bind what we do to what we think, action to belief, choice to judgment. It differs from true magical thought, which denies reason, in that it suspends but does not deny reason. By doing so, quasi-magical thought also suspends a *causal* nexus between our decisions and the reasons we give for making them. Tversky and Shafir's experiments open up a spyhole into what might happen in time: the abyss of a *kind* of irrationality, so far undervalued or kept well concealed.

No one believes that she can undo what is done or that she can turn back the clock and alter history. To do so would be magical thought, with no "quasi-" about it. The great theologians of the past agreed that even an omnipotent God could not do so. But when we don't know *what* course events have taken, what irreversible decisions have been made, then quasi-magical thought works within us to make us act, against reason, in such a way as to *simulate* in our actions the way our hearts wish events had taken place. We know that by acting in this way nothing will change, but nonetheless. . . . We do not act in such a way as to optimize the chances of real success, but to optimize the success we *would have had* had matters gone as we hoped.

Looking about us, we can see many examples of this sort of quasi-magical thought. One example, well known to psychologists and economists, will suffice: the enormous reluctance with which we "return to zero," to cut our losses (due to decisions made in the past) in order to make a fresh start. Against all rational calculation, we act as though we could exploit those past losses—not according to how our business is going or what might happen, but according to how it *would have gone* if we'd made the right decisions in the first place. We act by projecting our desires; we look for protection in regret and not in accordance with our most rational estimate of an effective reality.

Tversky and Shafir have also verified the power of the disjunctive effect in retrospect, by reconstructing the behavior of the stock market immediately before and after the presidential elections of 1988. Interviews, major articles, indices, and market surveys clearly show that the forecast (though for different reasons) was for an economic downturn, whether Bush or Dukakis won. Nonetheless, before the election, as before most elections, the market was in fact paralyzed, to recover only *after* the election. A similar phenomenon was observable in 1992. Here, though, most forecasts suggested a (mini-) recovery, whatever the result of the election. (In fact President Clinton benefitted from an initial mild recovery to which he had certainly not contributed.)

In other experiments, Tversky and Shafir have posed "electoral" questions to their subjects, looking at certain model scenarios and varying, against the whole electorate, the percentage of uncertain voters and sure voters. In times of political uncertainty, when their subjects feel that in that given situation it is vital that as many voters as possible actually do vote, they declare themselves sure to vote, in spite of the imagined discomfort caused by their personal act of voting. If the scenario is altered, and a model is proposed in which actually voting would still represent a high personal cost but it is not very important that many people do actually express their vote, the subjects then declare that they are less disposed to go and cast their own single vote. Thus these well-planned voting scenarios demonstrate the force of quasi-magical thought.

If once again this seems a rather banal conclusion, it is because a few of us recognize that the act of voting has certain *intrinsically* paradoxical aspects. The bottom line from the point of view of game theory and decision psychology is that in no major election can a single elector seriously or rationally suppose that his vote *alone* is going to change anything whatever. That is a straightforward matter of numbers. The illustrious Italian sociologist Alessandro Pizzorno, a former professor at Harvard University, analyzed this phenomenon; he attributed the motive for voting not to the objective probability of being able to change anything but to a sense of responsibility and the feeling of "belonging" that is involved in the act of voting. Tversky and Shafir's data confirm this thesis, and enrich traditional sociology and political science with the cognitive factor of disjunction.

Their data on the prisoner's dilemma give the lie to certain older theories about decisions based on collective reciprocity—that is, the theory that justified the choice of cooperation as a means toward the greatest possible collective advantage, as against the advantage of a single player. These "collectivist" theories suggested that we should always cooperate, because by so doing we maximized the *overall* usefulness of the two rivals. This came about as a means to explain an old fact: the constant and not negligible number (about one-third of all subjects in many published experiments) who opted to cooperate at all costs. According to traditional psycho-economic theory, these were people who found their reward in the mere fact of cooperating, without regard to any selfish economic calculation. Tversky and Shafir proved the superior strength of the disjunction effect in explaining the choice to cooperate. In fact, this latter shows up strongest and summons the *greatest* number of cooperators, not when the subject *knows* that the other has cooperated, but when she does not know what the other has done. Despite all the psycho-economic explanations of the "collective spirit," what is at work here is not altruism, but the *presumed* weight of ignorance. I say "presumed" because, as we have seen, the decisions have already been made, and not "knowing" what the other has chosen should have no influence whatever on one's own decision. But according to Tversky and Shafir, most subjects are extraordinarily inclined to "spend" to know "something more" about their rival's decisions, even when it is totally clear to them that such information cannot possibly alter an outcome. As experiments can show, this further "information" becomes an end in itself, not a means to arrive at a more carefully thought-out and better-considered decision.

There is in fact nothing rational about spending money to know what decision my adversary has taken, when it has been well established that my decision will be exactly the same, *whatever* his decision. An irrational prudence pushes us toward delay, toward further investigation, to find things that, whatever these might be, should not influence our decision.

Irrational prudence causes a loss of money, time, or both. Therefore, it should be of interest to ministries of health, insurance companies, and the like, not to speak of we taxpayers (all of us potential, if not actual, patients) that psychologists have found many instances of irrational prudence in the health profession. A typical model situation is where there is the choice of two therapies or when there is a question of operating or not. With the help of leading experts in the world of medicine, cognitive scientists have created some highly realistic, fact-based scenarios. These offer symptoms and data *sufficient* to decide, but also leave the subject (often a genuine clinician, and sometimes an equally "genuine" subject who imagines himself to be the patient in question) the option of proceeding to "further" clinical analyses, such as radiology and so on, *before* deciding. The most recent results of decision psychologists show that these further tests, which undoubtedly are *generically* useful but cannot reasonably influence that particular decision, are eagerly demanded, and in perfectly good faith. In fact, many clinicians, not to speak of many who imagine themselves ill, decide to wait until they have such "further" and "relevant" data.

It is obvious that this disjunction effect has, without malice or any special interest on the part of the laboratories, an adverse effect on the healthcare budget and hospital expenses. As is typical of the cases we have already seen, and of others we are about to see, the "pure" cognitive effect combines with other factors and is set in motion by them. But that effect remains even when these other, less noble, even spurious, factors are eliminated. A whole world of studies, investigations, reports, meetings with specialists, and so on, all of them brought in to "improve" the decision-making process, is often utterly useless.

Even when personal interests—and passing the buck, the fear of responsibility, and dozens of like factors—are eliminated, there remains, hidden, fundamental, and little understood outside of cognitive science, the disjunction effect. Further, this blind spot is often shot through with doubtful motives, but these few indications should be enough to suggest that even when all else is removed, the tunnel of irrational prudence is an all too likely path. It is not too soon to learn how to avoid it.

CHAPTER 5

Calculating the Unknown,
or Bayes' Law

The road maps we ought to use to get around our mental tunnels may not be fully known, even to experts in the subject, but those that are known are highly detailed. It is time we took a bird's-eye look at these maps. Large-scale maps—the kind you spread out on engineers' and architects' drawing boards—exist, in the form of advanced texts in statistics, decision theory, and cognitive science. So far, these maps have been the special province of a few experts, and therefore have remained largely untouched in public libraries. If we want things to change, if we want those around us to begin avoiding these tunnels, it is time that these matters be set out in simple form and made accessible to the layperson.

Bayes' law has been mentioned often enough; now it is time to describe it, at least in summary form. For centuries humankind has known how to count, how to measure space, and how to weigh goods with precision, but it was not until the eighteenth century that we solved an enigma that must have been nagging at us since the beginning of time: how to calculate an unknown probability from known data, or how to predict the future on the basis of precise data from the past. If they've accomplished nothing else, the preceding chapters have certainly demonstrated that our normal intuitions are hardly a basis for solving this problem. To succeed, we would in fact have to *subvert* our intuitions.

In this context, Bayes' law (though, as we will see in a moment, it is a very simple little formula) is truly one of the most important discoveries of the human mind. It is now set out in all treatises on statistics, in encyclopedias, and in manuals on inductive logic. My purpose is to give the reader an intuitive notion of this law, and to show how Bayes' law for all its simplicity can free us from the tunnel of native probabilistic reasoning.

In daily life, we often find that we need to make decisions on the basis of incomplete information; we then have to obtain further data to correct or confirm our decisions. A typical instance is when we have to make a reasonable forecast of some event taking place in the future and, to do so, have to amass the greatest possible amount of information as to the *most probable* outcome. The most-studied model for this process is that of the scientist who offers a hypothesis, tests it, and then decides to what degree his tests confirm or deny his theory. His task is to calculate *exactly*, not just to guess, how probable it is that a theory or a hypothesis, *given all that we know*, is true.

One immediate application is to the doctor who uses tests to help her in diagnosis, and this can easily be extended to the business executive faced with making a decision and receiving further information (e.g., from market research, works inspections, stock market tips) on which he will base that decision. As we have seen, this sort of rational decision making also should be extended to the courts.

The essential elements of the Bayesian procedure are as follows:

1. A series of possible alternatives (which statisticians call "states of nature") that come *before* the decision and the gathering of further information.

2. The a priori probability assigned to each alternative, before verification or testing.

3. The degree of reliability and the predictive capacity of each test.

4. The results of the tests (inquiries, controls).

5. The probability assigned to each alternative a posteriori— after, and in the light of, all the tests and the further information gathered.

Bayes' classic law—named for the English divine and mathematician Thomas Bayes, who discovered the law in the mid-eighteenth century—states that the probabilities in (5) can be exactly calculated on the basis of data provided in (1) through (4). The ideally rational subject is one defined as a "Bayesian" subject. This means that the *only* rational method to minimize risk and maximize advantage is to adopt the Bayesian strategy. It is to say that we *must* ourselves become Bayesian subjects if we wish only to make the most rationally advantageous choices. Today we have mathematical theorems that show how Bayes' law (in the abstract and under ideal conditions) is the only way to make certain decisions wholly rational. Calculating future probabilities from past probabilities, as well as assessing the likelihood that a certain hypothesis or conjecture may be right on the basis of data we have reliably gathered, is called "induction." It must be stressed that both Bayesian and non-Bayesian theoreticians of induction agree on the *formula* discovered by Bayes. In fact, by now it is simply and elegantly derived in the textbooks, via short theorems, from the most basic laws of probability. (Great discoveries usually do appear "simple" and uncontroversial after the fact, and with the passing of time.) What theoreticians disagree about is the *amount of* insight one gains from applying this formula to *all* actual cases of induction. I will not delve into these subtleties, and proceed to give a very simple and intuitive account of the formula. Even the non-Bayesians bow to the formula's elegance and admit it is very important, though not vitally (and not "imperialistically") so. An intuitive way of understanding what Bayes' strategy is all about is expressed in the following spoken (approximate, but intuitively telling) reasoning.

For each state of nature, we begin by ascertaining the probability that the state will occur as a result of the test (that is, its a posteriori probability), multiplying the probability of verification (with or without test—our a priori probability) by the intrinsic reliability of the test (that is, by the probability the test will assign to that state of nature *as compared to all other* states of nature). But this is insufficient.

Intuition goes wrong in not compelling us to examine, as well, other important variables that are essential to Bayes' law, such as the likelihood, given the test, that other states of nature may also occur and the probability that any particular state of nature may occur, *even if the test is negative.*

Of course, there is a formula for all this: the formula (or law, or theorem) of Bayes. In order not to frighten the reader, for whom mathematical formulae may be anathema, I offer a more colloquial version.

The Rev. Thomas Bayes' Formula in Plain Words

The probability that a hypothesis (in particular, a diagnosis) is correct, given the test, is equal to:

> The probability of the outcome of the test (or verification), *given* the hypothesis (this is a sort of inverse calculation with respect to the end we are seeking), multiplied by the probability of the hypothesis in *an absolute sense* (that is, independent of this test or verification) and divided by the probability of the outcome of the test in an absolute sense (that is, independent of the hypothesis or diagnosis).

Neither more nor less.

I say "in an absolute sense" to give the formula a little drama, to lighten up the words. Concretely, these "absolute" probabilities are those that we feel we can rationally assign to the outcome of the test in and of itself, paying no heed whatsoever to our hypothesis or diagnosis, and respectively, in regard to our hypothesis, paying no heed to the outcome of the test. These are probabilities we can consider as being assigned a priori. Not because these probabilities are exactly as they were a thousand years ago, or when our universe began, but because they seem, rationally, to be calculable *prior to the verification or testing procedure and before we even formulate that particular hypothesis.* We often call this an "old" probability, as opposed to a "new"—that indeed offered by Bayes' law. These "old" probabilities may be calculated only a few hours or a few minutes before the test. The fact that they are a priori probabilities is perfectly compatible with their being calculated before the particular test (one that might be thought of as resolving and decisive) that interests us, but after a great number of other tests, as well as in the light of *other* hypotheses or diagnoses, equally but differently reasonable.

This is the most delicate and difficult part of the operation: One is seeking to calculate the probability of the hypothesis before, and independently of, the test, as well as to calculate the probable result of the test, independent of *that* particular hypothesis but taking into account other plausible alternatives. This requires rigor, but also flair, common sense, an acute intuition, a fair dose of expertise, and a refined imagination.

Thereafter, applying Bayes' formula is purely mechanical. A pocket calculator can give you the result, which consists of no more than a multiplication and a division. The grandeur of Bayes' law lies precisely in its great formal simplicity—but a simplicity that requires a highly intelligent mix of science and art when applied to concrete examples. In individual cases, it is difficult to insert the right ingredients or numbers in the formula. A mistake in the "base," the "old" or a priori probabilities, means that the law's wheels grind out numbers, and an "answer" quite without sense. The correct calculation of the "base" probabilities *in a given sector,* such as a medical specialty, requires years of study and the cumulative experience of thousands of analogous cases and tests, each patiently analyzed. But we are interested in very simple cases, in which these "base" probabilities are already *given* in the text of the problem.

The vital message here is that no one is *spontaneously* a Bayesian subject. I am not referring here to those knowingly non-rational strategies which we may decide to follow with real-life problems, such as rejecting the decision in toto, clinging to a tradition or to what has always been done in like cases, deciding to operate by intuition against all probability. Our mental tunnels demonstrate that we are not Bayesian subjects *even* when we think we are deciding matters in a rational and sensible manner, and taking into account the spectrum of probabilities intuitively calculated, before and after the test. Typical examples were the diagnostic test and the jury (both in Chapter 4, Tunnel 6). This, of course, means that we should learn to consciously evoke Bayes' law when making decisions.

The Fallacy of Near Certainty

Before we attempt to adopt the strategies of Bayes' law, let us consider again briefly the (non-Bayesian) intuitions that underlie our naive conclusions. Then we would find yet another cognitive illusion, that of "near certainty."

If the diagnostic test or the lady's testimony in court were 100 percent reliable, we would be *certain* that our subject had fallen prey to that illness and that the taxi was truly a blue one. "Therefore," our intuition tells us, a test that is 87 percent reliable offers us 87 percent certainty, and a witness who is 80 percent reliable allows us to be 80 percent sure.

This is not true. Here we are prey to two further capital and systematic mistakes: (1) a naive form of extrapolation and (2) the confusion among necessary conditions, sufficient conditions, and conditions that are both sufficient *and* necessary. In the world of probability one cannot, even where the reliability is very close to 100 percent (or absolute certainty)—such as 95 percent—extrapolate. An intuition that is correct at the absolute level of 100 percent is *no longer* correct in cases that lie "close" to that 100 percent limit. In fact, in the case of the test for the disease, looking aside from the ideal cases, there could easily be three different tests to determine the likelihood of a given disease, which are, respectively:

1. Positive in *all* the subjects who have that disease but *also* in some who do not. Here one finds 0 percent of "false negatives" but a significant number of "false positives."

2. Negative in *all* the subjects who do *not* have the disease but not *only* with these. Here we have 0 percent false positives but a certain number of false negatives.

3. Positive in *all* subjects who suffer from the disease and *only* for these subjects. This result is highly idealized and never realizable in practice. It follows that the test is *also* negative *only* for *all* subjects who do not suffer from the disease.

Only the purely Utopian third test is 100 percent reliable, and it is to *this* test—in which the conditions are sufficient for us to have a certain diagnosis—that we refer to as the premise of our fallacy. A single sufficient condition is enough, *alone*, to determine the truth of the hypothesis with certainty. If, on the other hand, we refer to the other two cases, it is soon obvious that there is no longer a sufficient condition. If we know nothing of the relative frequency of the false positives in (1) and the false negatives in (2), in terms of probability, there is no way in which we can *transfer* the validity of the test (or the testimony) and imagine a near certainty. This frequency will vary according to different populations, and it is here that we should pay special attention to base frequencies.

Also to be noted is that the first test is insufficiently discriminating. It singles out all those who are ill, but it also includes other subjects, whereas test 2 is too discriminating, in that it leaves out a number of subjects who should have been included. But the truth is that many of us are inclined to treat both (1) and (2) as 100 percent reliable, though we generally add some such phrase as *in their own way* or *in a certain sense.*

Our intuitions find it very difficult to make these vital distinctions; hence the reason we incur this fallacy. For some reason we do not realize that when we stray, *even a little,* from the ideal test 3, such as by passing to (1) or (2), or by not noting the lesser reliability in *both,* we no longer have a sufficient condition. All we have is a certain probabilistic correlation.

Here it is vital to emphasize that *probabilistic correlations are not "like" a somewhat less certain certainty.* Such correlations can be treated rationally only by Bayes' law.

	Illness Present	Illness Absent
Test positive	A	B
Test negative	C	D

A, B, C, and D may be probabilities, or they may be numbers from a whole population verified by clinical tests, in which case they will be expressed in percentages, even though the samples may be different at the base in each class of data.

Experience shows that for a great many people, including the better informed, the correlation between test and illness is often made *paying attention only to data furnished by A.* Many hold that A is (or is identical to, or expresses) *the* correlation. This is, of course, a serious error. One cannot base oneself only on A. What counts is the complex relationship among the four. For statistical purposes, the most important is the relationship (quotient) between A and the sum (A+B) and the relationship between C and the sum (C+D).

As we shall see in the "selection task" devised by Wason and Johnson-Laird (Appendix B, "The Selection Task and Cheater Detectors"), we tend to consider A highly important (for some of us, this is the *only* important datum), B as somewhat important, and C as not so important. Very few think D is *also* important. But in fact, in a correct Bayesian calculation of the probability of a diagnosis, given the test result, D has a determining weight.

It bears repeating that none of us is, spontaneously or intuitively, a Bayesian subject. We have to learn at least some rudiments of statistics to modify our intuitions. The trouble is that as Tversky, Kahneman, and many others have shown, even professional scientists and statisticians can be induced into error—with examples that are indeed more sophisticated than, but qualitatively perfectly equivalent to, these.

The Seven Deadly Sins

We have looked at recent discoveries in heuristics and mental tunnels or blind spots. I would now like to relate these more closely to everyday concerns, and to link the effects of the cognitive unconscious to those of the emotional, and of other forms of irrationality. Stepping aside from technical classifications, I have established an intuitive classification of the more serious and insidious perils that support our illusion of knowing. They are set out here, in a somewhat joking manner, as the Seven Deadly Sins:

1. Overconfidence
2. Illusory correlations (magical thinking)
3. Predictability in hindsight
4. Anchoring
5. Ease of representation
6. Probability blindness
7. Reconsideration under suitable scripts

They are set out here in such a way that the psychological cause of each is to be found in those of its predecessors and their interactions. In this chapter I alternate examples from life and specific experiments. To show how important it is to know about these sins, and how many human and material disasters could be avoided if we did not commit them, I also take some consequences of these sins to their extreme. Let us now look at them one by one.

Overconfidence

In a classic paper published in 1977 in the *Journal of Experimental Psychology*, Baruch Fischhoff, Paul Slovic, and Sarah Lichtenstein asked a large number of subjects to reply to a set of generic questions to which the answers were in fact *certain*, but not necessarily known by their subjects. These questions were of the type exemplified in Double or Quit or Trivial Pursuit, and the correct answers were readily available in any encyclopedia or statistical table. Typical questions included, "What is the capital of Ecuador?" or "On average, in the United States, do more people die annually from suicide or from homicide?" or "Three-quarters of the world's cocoa production comes from Africa or South America?" Each subject was asked to answer the question and then calibrate just how likely it was that his or her answer was correct. Thus a subject might answer "Quito" to the first question, and that he was absolutely, or nearly, or half, sure that Quito really was the capital of Ecuador.

In this way it is possible to measure the degree of confidence that each subject feels in his or her reply to a given question or series of questions. I won't waste time on the details of the method, save to say that the authors bravely brought it to a high, even byzantine, degree of precision and refinement. It will be noted that this method permits the experimenters to make a true calibration for each respondent, to compare that calibration with the subject's own, and then to determine for which questions the gap between the two calibrations is the greatest. These results can then be manipulated to obtain averages for many different subjects, for one class of questions, a subgroup, and so on.

The results obtained by Fischhoff, Slovic, and Lichtenstein show a widespread and persistent tendency to overconfidence. Subjects who gave wrong answers to 15 percent of the questions (and who should therefore have rated themselves at 85 percent) instead rated themselves as 100 percent sure of their answers. For some of their wrong answers, the subjects rated the likelihood of their being wrong at one in a thousand, in ten thousand, or even in a million.

The discrepancy between the reliability of the replies and the degree of overconfidence was so great and so widespread that the researchers sought out a new group of respondents and, before giving them the test, gave them a thorough tutorial preparation (with charts, slides, and so on) as to the real meaning of a probability of one in a thousand, one in ten thousand, and so on. This preliminary clarification has come to be known as "debiasing," a form of mental hygiene that seeks to reduce, or eliminate, biases. The overconfidence level in these subjects, as compared to those who had come to the tests unprepared, fell somewhat, but not very greatly. Debiasing turned out, in fact, to be a very, very difficult task.

Seeking to verify just how firmly their respondents backed their own overconfidence, the researchers asked the subjects if they were willing to bet real money on the correctness of their answers. The researchers' idea was as follows: If the subject maintained that the probability of her being wrong on a given answer was one in a thousand, then she should accept a bet that would reflect this probability. For instance, if the answer was wrong, she should be willing to bet at odds of 10 to 1, risking $10 to win $100. (Actually, she should be willing to bet at an even greater risk, such as 500 to 1.) To the researchers' great surprise, their respondents really were disposed to bet (modest) sums on their own evaluations. Some were in fact incensed when they learned that Fischhoff, Slovic, and Lichtenstein had, as a matter of fact, no intention of taking bets with real money.

One series of questions turned out remarkably anomalous. For these questions, the answers had the highest number of mistakes, but were backed by the highest degree of overconfidence. Here are some of them, as given to U.S. students.

Probable Causes of Mortality in the United States

Which of these causes of death do you think are statistically most frequent? (The confident answers were given with great confidence by a majority of the respondents; the correct answer appears on the right.)

Confident Answer	*Correct Answer*
Pregnancy, abortion, and childbirth combined	Appendicitis
All accidents of any kind	Heart attacks
Homicide	Suicide
Fireworks accidents	Measles
Suicide	Diabetes
Breast Tumor	Diabetes

General Knowledge Questions

Three-quarters of the world's production of cocoa comes from:

Confident Answer	*Correct Answer*
South America	Africa

When did the first ever aerial bombardment take place?

Confident Answer	*Correct Answer*
in 1937	in 1849

Adonis was the god of:

Confident Answer	Correct Answer
Love	Vegetation

Kahlil Gibran was principally inspired by:

Confident Answer	Correct Answer
Buddhism	Christianity

Dido and Aeneas *is an opera written by:*

Confident Answer	Correct Answer
Berlioz	Purcell

The potato originated in:

Confident Answer	Correct Answer
Ireland	Peru

These questions were not chosen with the purpose of confounding the respondents, but were discovered after the fact to have been particularly troublesome or deceptive to many. These questions also were found, after the fact, to have led to a far greater than average degree of overconfidence. The researchers decided, therefore, to make a separate classification of these questions and to recalibrate all the other questions *separately*, removing the troublesome group of questions.

This study, as well as others, shows that the discrepancy between correctness of response and overconfidence *increases* as the respondent is *more knowledgeable*. Those who know less have a reduced level of overconfidence. On the other hand, when the answer is more elaborate, requires considerable reasoning, and is based on specialized knowledge, the level of accuracy increases, yes, but the level of overconfidence increases to a far greater degree.

It is therefore most important to be wary of our overconfidence, for this over-confidence is *at its greatest* in our own area of expertise—in short, just where it can do the most damage.

Magical Thinking

This deadly sin is generally linked to the lesser (though not merely venial) sin of quasi-magical thinking (see Chapter 4, "It's Not True, but I Believe It: Quasi-Magical Thinking"). As we have seen, a statistical correlation is not a near certainty, or a slightly less "certain" certainty; it is something else altogether. The blind spot revealed by our clinical test (see Chapter 4, Tunnel 6) demonstrated that conclusively. The statistical correlation between a clinical test and a diagnosis (between a "sign" and an actual phenomenon, between a test and a fact, etc.) depends on a whole constellation of data and a well-ordered series of quantitative considerations.

It has been established that the majority of subjects without statistical know-how (but not just these) tend to assimilate the correlation to the incidence of the illness *only* in the case of positive cases. Let's look back at the table we made, which contained a single symptom and a single diagnosis:

		Illness	
		Present	Absent
Symptom	Present	A	B
	Absent	C	D

Basing oneself only on A, there is the illusion of a correlation; one falls victim to "magical thinking." Suppose you are asked to verify the following diagnostic hypothesis: Persons suffering from delusions of persecution (even in a mild form) tend to draw the human face with very large or pronounced eyes. To verify this hypothesis, you have but to examine a series of psychological profiles, each with a set of drawings, made spontaneously. For simplicity's sake, let's imagine that these drawings are on index cards. On one side is the psychological profile of the subject, and on the other is a characteristic drawing made by the same respondent (or a series of drawings at a reduced size). Now four *kinds* of cards are laid before us on a table, in such a way that we can only see one of the two sides of each card. These cards show:

1. A psycho-portrait indicating persecution mania
2. Another psycho-portrait that does not mention any such mania
3. A drawing with exaggerated eyes
4. Another drawing with normal eyes

Let us now ask ourselves which cards we absolutely must turn over to check the correctness of our hypothesis. It is clearly necessary not to turn over those cards that are useless to the hypothesis or that do not lend themselves greatly to such a verification. We are in fact trying to maximize the efficiency of our control by making the *minimum* possible number of checks.

Two English psychologists, Peter Wason and Philip Johnson-Laird, examined a great number of these problems, known as "selection tasks." It emerged from their study that nearly all their respondents chose to turn over card (1), which they considered crucial; many also indicate that (3) is also important; few mention (2) and almost no one (to be precise, usually less than 10 percent) picks (4). The simplest logical calculation, based on the table of validity of the "logical functions," called "conditionals" (approximately corresponding to the expression "if . . . then . . ." in ordinary language), shows that only (1) and (4) are really worth looking at.

In fact, this hypothesis is quickly verified by turning the cards over. The hypothesis is wrong if on the other side of (1) there is a drawing without exaggerated eyes; similarly, the hypothesis is wrong if on the other side of (4) we find a psychological profile that indicates persecution mania. The other two cards are totally irrelevant for purposes of verification or disproval of the hypothesis. In fact, the hypothesis does not suggest (and it would be absurd to say so) that *only* those suffering from persecution mania make drawings with exaggerated eyes, nor does it suggest that *all* drawings with exaggerated eyes are made *only* by those suffering from such a mania.

The same cards, with the same database of clinical diagnoses, can be used to show that an unsophisticated respondent is every bit as readily induced to believe the opposite hypothesis: Those who suffer from persecution mania draw faces with small or unremarkable eyes. Nor will the subject limit himself to that: He is able to explain why this should be so. In the first case he will argue that sufferers from persecution mania draw faces with large eyes because they feel they are constantly spied upon; in the second, he will advance the thesis that they draw faces with small eyes because they are afraid to look into other people's eyes, or because by so doing they are exorcising their fear of being constantly observed.

There is a psychological law that has been endlessly confirmed, even among professionals and experts, among doctors, psychiatrists, judges, teachers, insurers, engineers, meteorologists, and so forth:

> When someone is convinced of a positive correlation, however illusory that correlation can objectively be shown to be, that person will always find new confirmations and justify why it should be so.

We now know how to pick out the subjective factors, the heuristics, and the mental tunnels or blind spots that underlie this deadly sin of intuitive judgment: our tendency to overlook base frequencies, to skip over those cases that falsify our correlations, and our inability accurately to calculate a correlation rationally, in its complex whole. A well-known philosopher of science, Karl R. Popper, found fame with his hypothesis that the hypotheses of science can be falsified, but not verified. Without going into the rights and wrongs of Popper's position, we can at least conclude that if this is so—that is, that the proper method for science is to proceed by refutation rather than by confirmation—then scientific method makes a break with our spontaneous intuition. As dozens of tests with selection tasks have shown, whether the scenarios these offer are familiar or abstract, whether they refer to injunctions or social contracts, we are naturally and spontaneously verifiers rather than falsifiers or debunkers. This is especially true when dealing with generalized or abstract hypotheses, such as those that are genuinely scientific. If we want to become Popperians, then we have to revolutionize our spontaneous intuitions and learn to distrust our magical thinking. The next deadly sin reveals a particularly interesting and exasperating instance of this kind of thinking.

Predictability in Hindsight

The typical experiment in this domain asks a subject how probable it is, given certain premises or symptoms or signs, that he or she might have foreseen a certain event we know actually happened. The subject is supplied with the following: (1) a precise description of an event that *certainly* did happen (the outbreak of a conflict, galloping inflation, an ecological disaster, a company failure, the huge success of a given product) and (2) a series of relevant pieces of information available *before* the event.

Cognitive psychologists sometimes have to be perverse for professional reasons, and they enjoy turning the tables on their respondents. Thus to some subjects they give real prior data and then the resulting event, whereas they give others the same data but a directly *opposite* result. (Naturally, even in the latter case, the subjects are always told that the pairings of data and outcomes are correct.) The psychologists then tabulate the level of confidence with which their respondents, afforded the relevant data, think they could have predicted the result. They also analyze their subjects' justifications, as well as the reasoning the subjects used to reach their conclusions, and so on.

It turns out that with hindsight we all honestly think we could have predicted what happened, *as long as we know, or think we know, that it actually did happen.* The researchers found no difference at all in the confidence between those furnished with the true sequence of events and those who were given (without being told) the opposite result. When the same kinds of pairings between data and outcomes were presented as "educated guesses" about *future* events the subjects' confidence decreased dramatically. Being told that we know for sure that the outcome *did* indeed happen has the power to produce what is called "predictability in hindsight." It is tempting to connect this tunnel of the mind with the disjunction effect (see Chapter 4, Tunnel 8). For obvious reasons, historians are particularly prone to commit this sin.

To the great distaste of historians, psychologists have revealed many typical fallacies in the ancient and honorable art of history, the so-called historian's fallacies. I list below merely a few of the historical sophistries psychologists have uncovered:

- The diary of an "acute" observer of the period contains the phrase: "Today the Hundred Years War began."

- I will now show you why Napoleon *had* to know that he would lose the Battle of Waterloo.

- There may be one weak hypothesis, one weak link in the chain of my reasoning, but all the other links are very strong. As we know that what I propose in my historical scheme is effectively true, then this hypothesis, too, *must* be true.

- In fact what actually happened was exactly the opposite of what I had predicted in my 1978 article, but I can tell you precisely why by using the very method I used before.

- What my esteemed colleague predicted turned out to be correct, but that is a matter of pure chance, for I can *prove* that the model he used is entirely wrong.

There's no point is chiding historians to excess; economists, political scientists, politicians, doctors, and generals all make the same mistake. Let he or she who is without sin cast the first stone.

On the other hand, we should not overlook the disastrous results of this cognitive illusion. One doesn't have to take up the case of the cynical and merciless way in which politics must always find a scapegoat: It can be scientifically demonstrated that this predictability in hindsight strikes at even the best balanced and well-intentioned people. An unfortunate victim can be fired, his or her career blocked, or worse under the pernicious effect of this illusion. Even sadder is the fact that it won't be particularly difficult to convince the victim that in fact he or she *should have* been able to predict what happened on the basis of the data he or she had available. As in the noted servant-master dialectic of Hegel, in which the slave ends up being persuaded by his master that he *had* to be and should be a slave, the scapegoat is persuaded that he could, indeed *should*, have foreseen what would happen.

The next sin is closely related.

Anchoring

We have already taken note of one precise and striking example of this sin, in rapid multiplication (see Chapter 3). Another classic experiment consists in asking a subject, for instance, how many African nations there are in the United Nations. Before asking him that question, however, one turns the wheel

of fortune in full view of the subject, stopping it on some number between 1 and 100. You can tell your subject until you're
blue in the face that the number that turns up on the wheel
and the number of African states in the United Nations have
nothing in common, yet the result, on average, is the same:
The number of African states will be anchored to the number
turned up by the wheel of fortune. If, say, 12 comes up, the
number will always be smaller than if the wheel stops on, say,
92. It may seem incredible, but it's true.

Propagandists know all about this phenomenon, and it
was ably used by the Bush administration during the Gulf War.
The usual bulletin that followed an allied air raid would speak
of two, three, or a dozen Iraqi civilian victims. Skeptical as one
might be (and I was skeptical) about the accuracy of these figures, one's mental adjustment of that figure upward always
remained anchored to those first numbers. In our hearts we
may have multiplied them by 10 or even by 100, but not by
10,000, as it turns out we should have. Only many months after
the campaign did we begin to hear about tens upon tens of
thousands of victims. This may be a recent instance; the practice is as old as history.

At the opposite end of the scale, every good police officer
in the world (and some husbands or wives, suspicious or jeal-
ous) knows how effective it is to accuse someone of multiple
and infamous crimes. Under such a torrent of accusations and
presumed "proofs," the poor victim ends up "conceding" that,
yes, it's true that . . . but all the rest is utterly false. The accused
does everything he can to "anchor" the accusations against
him to a much smaller number of less important crimes, seeking to form an umbrella that might protect him against the del-
uge of worse crimes of which he's accused. Of course, this little
concession is just what the prosecutor wanted to hear. The
"anchoring" effect gives a sinister force to even the most
unsupported calumny. Innocent phrases such as "there's no
smoke without fire" combine this deadly sin with others equally
well known: envy, pride, hatred.

An extensive scientific literature deals with such cases in the courts, and in hospitals, not to speak of collective decisions that reflect the perilous infiltration of this anchoring effect. We are especially affected when we are forced to make a spur-of-the-moment judgment, in which case we tend to perform a kind of self-anchoring. Revising an intuitive, impulsive judgment will never be sufficient to undo the original judgment completely. Consciously or unconsciously, we always remain anchored to our original opinion, and we correct that view only starting from that same opinion. Anchoring here is given full backing by pride and self-satisfaction.

Though I've never done any work in personnel, it seems to me that one never *completely* undoes first impressions. It strikes me as not particularly rational to think this is not so. To grow more conscious of this in ourselves is one way to reduce the damage done by this sin.

Ease of Representation

If you compare the actual statistics for the causes of mortality in the United States with the opinions as to the causes (generally erroneous, but delivered with abundant confidence), you will find that this sin figures prominently. The number of Americans dead of diabetes is markedly greater than those dying from fireworks accidents, but the vast majority of people think the opposite. Why? Primarily because fireworks accidents are reported in the newspapers and remain impressed on our memory. No newspaper speaks of death from diabetes.

The same is true of suicides (only a few of which are reported) as against murders (which are fewer, but much more notorious.) Examples can be multiplied. Long ago, Bertrand Russell identified the force behind "popular inductions," which are kinds of spontaneous generalizations: These are based on the emotional nature of the examples, not on their objective number. To state this rule in slightly different terms:

> The easier it is to imagine an event or a situation, and the more
> the occurrence impresses us emotionally, the more likely we
> are to think of it as also objectively frequent.

For instance, we slow down a bit as soon as we have seen or
heard about an automobile accident. The accident we saw, or
had described to us vividly by someone we know well, does not
make it any more likely objectively that we, too, will have an
accident. This is, obviously, an instance of powerful synergies
between cognitive and emotional factors. In many cases, we
simply adopt the easiest strategies, the ones we can most
readily imagine. Because fireworks are more vivid than diabetes, we assign them a higher risk. Hence the term *ease of repre-*
sentation. In spite of the programmatic and self-administered
anesthesia of the cognitive scientist vis-à-vis the emotions, this
mental tunnel merges with tunnels of a different kind. The
emotional factors, so rightly emphasized even by Bertrand Russell, possibly the purest of logicians and one of the most dispassionate thinkers of modern times, have to be taken into
account. The accident suddenly and vividly reminds us of our
neglect of due safety precautions. We are caught defenseless
against a perfectly justifiable sense of guilt. The job of the cognitive scientist here is to show that such emotional factors,
important as they are, do not *suffice* to explain these phenomena. Our overrating of the actual frequency of, say, deaths due
to fireworks accidents versus deaths due to diabetes, or of
homicides versus suicides, cannot be accounted for by emotional factors alone.

Our ease of representation and our emotional involvement do combine, but the first may well *remain* enhanced even
when the second goes back to its "normal" level. Typically,
when planning a trip, one takes precautions against those risks
that are easiest for us to imagine, not against those that are
objectively most frequent. A standard nineteenth-century conversation manual for German tourists in Italy duly contained a
chapter on what to say in case one was incarcerated by mistake.

Clearly, the ease of imagination of the average tourist varies significantly over time. Modern editions do not contain such chapters, in spite of the fact that in the recent past, mostly because of terrorism and drug-related crimes, the objective probability of mistaken arrest has, if anything, increased.

Having now stressed the cognitive component, because it's the one of which we have very little awareness, we must conclude that this capital sin in all its sinister power is indeed an inextricable amalgam of cognitive and emotional factors. They are both irrational, but the first masquerades more easily as rational, or semirational. A redeeming feature is that sudden boosts in our ease of representation, and sharp occasional reminders that we do care a lot for someone or something, often serve the noble purpose of inducing us to correct habits and neglects that are even *more* irrational and damaging.

Doctors, managers, and decision makers should take particular care not to fall into this frightening trap. The mortality rates tell us just how great is the difference between our mental images of probability and the objective facts. Things that seem "odd" to us are anything but. Curious "coincidences" turn out to be perfectly ordinary. The mathematician Persi Diaconis of Harvard has published extensively on this phenomenon, and Amos Tversky recently disproved a universally perceived idea that great basketball players develop a "hot hand." Here is a simple example of how we go wrong in considering a "curious" coincidence.

> What is the minimum number of persons there should be
> in a meeting room for there to be a better than 50 percent
> chance that two of them have the same birthday?

The correct answer is in "Tunnel Exits." I guarantee you will be surprised!

Think of a CEO, a doctor, a general, or a cabinet minister who thinks she has discovered an alarming series of "coincidences," and who consecrates much time and many resources to discovering why. A good example is offered by the "conspiracy theorists" studying the Kennedy assassination. They argue that the deaths of a number of people involved, however remotely, with either the Kennedys, Oswald, or Jack Ruby are related to the assassination. In fact their coincidences might, I say might (this would require a full-blown statistical calculation), be just like the cabinet minister's. They might be no more than events that fit the natural, objective frequency statistics. Given the capital sins we have examined so far, there is no doubt that the cabinet minister will find the "cause," and will make completely irrational, and sometimes harmful, decisions based upon the discovery.

It is absolutely vital that all of us become wary of this elementary and universal factor in human nature. Objective statistical frequency is one thing; the facility with which our imagination represents certain events or situations, and our emotional impressionability, are quite another. Often we come across "coincidences" that in fact have nothing strange about them at all; in those cases we should not go fishing for "plots" or for "the guilty."

Probability Blindness

The case of the unknown virus and the vaccine (Chapter 4, Tunnel 7) shows that we are disposed to pay more for something that reduces risk to zero from one in a thousand than for something that reduces it to one in a thousand from two, or to three from four in a thousand. As I pointed out about the test for the illness, there is a threshold below which probabilities come at the same price. A probability of 9 in 1,000 and 5 in 10,000 costs the same. At the extreme opposite is a lottery with a very limited desirable prize. A sheet of tickets that give us a 99 percent chance of winning will be preferred to a more expensive sheet that offers a 999 per 1,000 chance. At the extremes, probability makes very little difference to us.

The same blindness is evident when we acquire "extra" lottery tickets: Those that increase our chance of winning from 32 to 37 percent (an advantage that we find very marginal) are considered far less interesting than those that increase our chances from 94 to 99 percent. But the advantage in probability is constant: 5 percent. As we have seen, no one would buy an insurance policy against fire that was good for only two weeks in any month, even if such a policy cost one-quarter of what a full policy cost. But this would be the more rational choice if the doubling of the risk cost one-quarter of a full policy.

We are, therefore, blind not only to extremes of probability, but also to intermediate probabilities—from which one might well adduce that we are blind about probability.

There is a lot of truth in this only slightly pessimistic statement. The truth is that we are impressed by nothing less than *big* differences in probability, and only when those occur at either pole (near certainty and near-certainly not). We all understand perfectly well the difference between a 3 percent probability that we will suffer a financial disaster and the certainty (e.g., thanks to an insurance policy) that we will not suffer such a disaster at all. We understand far less well the difference between this "certainly not" and a risk represented by a probability of 1 in 10,000. The fact is that many of us want to have (such as when we face doctors) insurance that guarantees no risk at all. If there is risk, but an extremely limited risk, such as 1 in 10,000, we are worried by the fact that there is a risk of some sort, as though between a risk of 1 in 10,000 and a risk of 1 in 100, there were almost no difference at all.

We need only think of the angry arguments against genetic engineering or for and against nuclear power, or the rigorous controls placed on the marketing of new pharmaceuticals, to understand just how blind we are when it comes to extreme probabilities. That peremptory desire that there be no risk at all has no rational basis, and scientific progress has been, and will continue to be, impeded by this collective irrationality. I've often heard people ask whether this or that new scientific theory is "absolutely" true, or whether some new technology is without risk. Faced with a frank and rational admission that there is no such thing as absolute certainty, such people say, "In that case we shouldn't really trust it," just as though a one-in-a-million risk were the same as a 50 percent risk.

In short, *public opinion holds that there either is risk or there isn't.* And if there is risk, it doesn't matter what or how great (or small) it is. I have no illusions that this is a pure cognitive illusion, or that what is wrong here is simply heuristics and blind spots. A lot else is involved: our emotions, our fear of science, immobilism, resistance to novelty, plain ignorance, and so on.

Still, I would like to warn against certain better balanced and more subtle forms of probability blindness. I would like to suggest a simple, general, probabilistic law:

> Any probabilistic intuition by anyone not specifically tutored in probability calculus has a greater than 50 percent chance of being wrong.

In other words, it is always more likely that our probabilistic intuition will be wrong than it is right. Let us therefore be wary of interpreting statistics in improvised fashion, and of estimates of probability made by ourselves or by others, unless these have been advanced with great care by professionals in the science of statistics.

I am not simply warning against the mystifying use of statistics by "authorities" that are hardly authoritative or by manipulative international "experts." There's worse than that. I am warning us against the naive way in which we read statistics that seem totally indisputable, that are literally bomb-proof. Countless examples exist, and we have seen a few cases of perfectly reliable statistics from which we have, in good faith, drawn erroneous conclusions.

Let us now pass to the seventh, and perhaps the deadliest, of our sins.

Reconsideration under Suitable Scripts

In the middle of the Polish crisis, in the early 1980s, while there were riots over the high cost of living and the lack of food, Tversky and Kahneman asked a number of political leaders and generals to evaluate the probability that the United States might withdraw its ambassador from the then Soviet Union (without any hypothesis as to why). They further asked the same subjects to evaluate the probability that *both* of two other things would take place: (a) that the U.S.S.R. would invade Poland and (b) that, as a consequence of the former, the United States would withdraw its ambassador from the Soviet Union.

This case is identical to that of Linda and Bill (see Chapter 4, Tunnel 3). This is the conjunction effect: the way in which we think it more likely that two or more things will happen together than that one of these, without regard to the other (which may or may not happen), will take place. This is simply irrational, for the *joining* of two events is always less likely than that each one of them will happen by itself. The overall probability of two events happening is always less than the *least* of the two single probabilities. What was going on in these people's minds? The event had become more probable because it was more readily presentable, easier to imagine. But what was it that made it so much easier to imagine? A scenario, a script, a fable, a form of pure fantasy!

A very clear recent example that such scripts can have a major influence on our lives was published by the *New York Times* on 17 February 1992. The headline reads: "The Pentagon sees new enemies to fight after the Cold War." Drastic cuts in the military budget had been approved, and had forced the Pentagon (in order to protect those budgets) to invent the following war scenarios, all of which are, though purely imaginary, more or less plausible.

1. Iraq invades Kuwait and Saudi Arabia.
2. North Korea attacks South Korea.

3. Both invasions occur simultaneously.

4. Russia attacks Lithuania via Poland, assisted by Byelorus.

5. A coup d'etat in the Philippines threatens the lives of 5,000 American residents.

6. A coup d'etat in Panama blocks access to the Panama Canal.

7. A new superpower with atomic capability and expansionist aims emerges.

The Pentagon itself recognized that these scenarios were neither inevitable nor imminent; they were simply "illustrations." What did appear imminent and inevitable in the military's eyes was a real need for an increase in defense spending through 1993–1994. Whatever the fate of these matters would be in the hands of a new administration, it is clear that "possible, futuristic scenarios" projected over a 10-year period were used to urge the U.S. treasury to pour out billions of real, immediate dollars.

Here is deadly sin number 7 in its most blatant form, in that our judgment of probability allows itself to be influenced by fictions, including scenarios that we know to be the fruit of pure invention. I call this the Othello effect. You may remember that the lustful and thwarted Iago sets out to make Othello believe his beloved wife, Desdemona, is unfaithful to him. Iago makes up a scenario involving Desdemona's handkerchief. This plausible but fallacious scenario convinces Othello of Desdemona's betrayal, and in a fury of passion, Othello kills her. Such fictitious scenarios can be taken advantage of by any shrewd and unscrupulous Iago.

But before we seek to save Desdemona, let us go back a few years to when Tversky and Kahneman ran their experiment on the Polish situation. Let's imagine a much stranger possibility than the withdrawal of the U.S. ambassador to the Soviet Union. How likely do you think it is that the United States might invade Poland? Here the chances are in the order of one in a million or less. But supposing we ask our respondents to consider the following sequence of events (you have to think yourself back into those times): Strikes in Poland intensify; crowds are fired on; Lech Walensa is imprisoned; the pope goes to Warsaw on a peace mission and is arrested; world public opinion is inflamed; the United States sends a specialist force to free the Pope. . . .

As the narrative unfolds one event is linked with another, making for a script that seems plausible—always admitting, of course, that each stage has really been preceded by another. In the end, don't we think that the probability of a U.S. invasion is somewhat higher than one in a million?

Here we leave statistics behind and enter the domain of pure fiction. Look a bit closer, and one can see that we are not yet out of the realm of cognitive science, for these question-naire-experiments, just like real life, have countless times shown us that a plausible and well-told story can lead us to hold as "objectively" probable events that, just minutes before, we would have considered totally improbable. The notorious "Protocols of Zion," a pure fabrication of the czar's anti-Semitic propaganda taken up by the Nazi regime raised an anti-Semitic storm. It did little good to show that it was a pure invention. What the propagandists sought to do, in order to seize power, was to make imaginatively presentable the proba-bility of a worldwide Jewish conspiracy, and in so doing they succeeded admirably, at least in the minds of those uncritically committed to hatred. I will not waste space on other instances, but limit myself to the purely cognitive aspects of the phenom-enon.

Offering a "plausible" sequence of events that are causally linked one to another has the effect of immediately raising our estimate of probability. It suffices that the links between these "events" should hold *from one to the next* for our minds to approach the final link in the chain. For, as we have seen, that which we can readily imagine is *ipso facto* more probable. Even if the probability of the very first link in this chain is very low, the fact is soon forgotten. Say "Let's suppose that . . ." and we're off, putting together a series of consequences, all of them "plausible" enough. I put "plausible" in quotation marks because true plausibility, in effect, depends *wholly* on that initial "Let's suppose . . ." Once the first link in the chain of our script is "supposed," then all the rest of the links "hold" one to another.

Rationally speaking, however, and having regard to the calculation of probabilities, we are in the domain of what is known as "compound probabilities," or, more restrictively, "conditional probabilities." (What is the likelihood that B will be true, *supposing* that A has proven to be true?) The probability of the last link in the chain being true is calculated on the basis of a series of conditional probabilities being true, and that in turn is obtained by *combining* the probabilities of each link in the chain, from the first to the last. Probabilities being, by their nature, less than one, the probability of the entire chain (or the last link) being true is *always and without exception less probable than the probability of the least probable link in the chain.*

We fail to notice this progressive attenuation of probability. The story takes over from reality. The last link seems ever truer to our mind, and our increased facility in representing or imagining makes that last link seem ever more probable. The trick—which is one of the oldest in the book—is to find the narrative path by which the last, *and most implausible,* link can be made imaginatively compelling. My Othello effect depends on this perverse use of the imagination.

If by chance one or two of the intervening links in this chain should come true, then poor Desdemona will indeed die. A narrative chain put together with art by some cunning Iago, and "resting" on a pair of intermediate links that come true (though only true for quite different reasons, and for reasons that no one may know), becomes irresistible. Poor us! The narrative then becomes an impregnable "logical" demonstration. Iago can transform doubt into certainty. Iago is not acting in good faith, and Othello, truth to tell, is no Sherlock Holmes. A rational, rigorously deductive man, knows perfectly well that the deductive inferences Iago makes about Desdemona's fidelity don't amount to much. His "indications," hints, and "proofs" could all be explained without the infidelity hypothesis. Bayes' law, or for that matter any sensible use of compound probability calculations, can save Desdemona from a horrible and unjust fate.

Instead, reinforced by our cognitive illusions and dark passions, by a *single* imaginary chain of "plausibilities," and by a pair of intermediate links that for totally unrelated reasons are true, Desdemona's tragic death is set into motion. The implausible becomes plausible, indeed certain. Give us a little story, a script, something born of our own imagination, and our own natural tendencies, cognitive or emotional, do the rest. Isn't this really the deadliest of our deadly sins?

If we combine these seven deadly sins, or take them each separately, and if we then feed them our own prejudices, our passions, our less than noble motives, one winds up with a rather desolate vision of the psychological bases for a great part of human behavior. One might even arrive at a serious devaluation of human rationality. Nonetheless, it remains true that a first important step is taken the moment we shed light on these built-in defects in our judgment, these illusions about knowing. It is only a first step, because the cognitive revolution is still in its infancy, its rhythm of research is still comparatively slow, and we are far from having exhausted what we might still discover.

CHAPTER 8

How to Emerge from the Tunnel of Pessimism

L et us draw up a balance sheet of what we have learned so far about our cognitive unconscious. Without any guilt on our part, simply because we are a part of the human species, all of us come into the world with certain mental eyeshades (we call them biases, tunnels, or blind spots), and we tend to act according to certain tricks (or heuristics), about which we know at least a part, to get ourselves out of certain binds. The effects of these heuristics and these blind spots are only partly perceived by us, and they are all subsumed under the generic name of "cognitive illusions." At this point we know enough to affirm that cognitive illusions are:

> **General**, because they are found in all human beings, or at least in a clear majority of normal, "naive" (that is, not specifically trained to be wary of *those* particular illusions) subjects.

Systematic, because they can be almost exactly reproduced in many situations to which they are related by kind, even if not always by level of complexity.

Directional, because their effects always tend in one direction (anchoring, rounding off, framing, segregation, etc.) and therefore are not simply fluctuations of opinion that might pull us now this way, now that.

Specific, because they are found in problems and choices with certain particular characteristics, and not in any and all human affairs.

Externally modulable, because the cunning experimenter can sharpen or attenuate them in a systematic and foreseeable fashion, scientifically varying both the nature of the problem and the way in which it is presented.

Subjectively incorrigible (at least to a point), because "telling" the subject that he is spontaneously inclined to commit certain errors does not immediately lead him to cease doing so (those who don't believe me should await perusal of my grand finale).

Nontransferable, because even knowing that one is inclined to commit certain errors in certain kinds of problems is insufficient to make us immune to error when we face problems that are only superficially different.

Independent of intelligence and education, because economists, mathematicians, and acknowledged experts are qualitatively subject to the same cognitive illusions as the novice when the apparent difficulty of the problem is increased.

All these traits merit the term *illusion* and reduce the distance between cognitive and perceptual illusions (in particular, the classic optical illusions). They also show that we are discovering something deep in human nature, and not just a trite statement of "human stupidity."

It is in fact important to distinguish carefully between cognitive illusions and simple errors of judgment or blunders due to inattention, distraction, lack of interest, poor preparation, genuine stupidity, timidity, braggadocio, emotional imbalance, and so on. Without exception, we have limited ourselves to a group of subjects psychologically and intellectually normal, attentive, and motivated but not under stress (nothing was at stake in the replies received, neither careers, money, dignity, nor anything else). It should be emphasized that cognitive science consists of probing the ordinary mental structures of the human species, free from such spurious effects as might be due to motivation, emotions, or aggressivity. Cognitive illusions are a new chapter not merely in our scientific knowledge, but also in our knowledge about ourselves. Cognitive illusions are the "frontier" of cognitive science, the border along which the psychology of the spontaneous touches on logic, the philosophy of mind and epistemology, collective convention, and mores, beliefs, and prejudices in the most traditional sense.

By their very nature, cognitive illusions offer us alarming scientific data, for these illusions influence our choices and our judgments even in cognitively and emotionally *ideal* situations. Cognitive illusions, unknown to science until some 20 years ago, are active in all of us, even when we are relaxed, attentive, and well disposed, with nothing to win or lose. Ideological, racial, social, or chauvinistic prejudices, as well as aggressive or prevaricatory instincts, can augment and exploit these cognitive illusions, but even if these are perverting factors, illusions will still be present and active. As we have seen, these illusions almost always work without our knowledge.

It is therefore important to clarify just how cognitive illusions are distinct from the *ordinary* limits of our rationality—from those limits classically defined as being due to our lack of omniscience, the incompleteness of our information, the unforeseeable fluctuations of phenomena, our limited capacity for abstraction, the limits of scientific knowledge, and so on. Fortunately, there exists a powerful and long-standing corpus of *normative* theories that enable us to create the backdrop against which the existence and nature of cognitive illusions can be made clear.

Optical illusions or mirages are considered fallacious because we have the means with which to verify that in an objective reality, *things are not as they seem.* The astronomer is *certain* that there are no heavenly bodies whose volume actually increases as they seem, in line with the horizon, to "cross" certain zones in space, and that this *must* therefore be an optical illusion. In the Müller-Lyer figure (see Chapter 1), anyone can measure the two segments with a ruler and verify that they are indeed equal. Physics, geometry, mathematics, probability calculus, logic, and the theory of measurement are, even at their most elementary (or naive) levels, a reliable basis on which to build our sense of reality and our rationality. When we note something superficially different from an objectively measurable reality, or from the known laws of the exact sciences, we do not thereby conclude that logic, mathematics, or science is wrong; we understand that we are suffering from an illusion.

The cognitive scientist is equally *certain* that the normative principles of rationality are not subverted when we make choices and judgments incompatible with those principles. The *systematic* failure of many of our "judgments under uncertainty" is not argument against the canons of rationality, but rather a demonstration that we frequently, without being aware of it, adopt strategies and mental intuitions that vary quite a bit from the formulas prescribed by those rational rules. These variations are not an alternative to rationality, nor are they a form of "alternative rationality." The age of "alternative" solutions is fortunately over. Today we should neither deny nor diminish the importance of these discoveries, nor should we disavow the values of true rationality. We have come to see that our minds spontaneously follow a sort of quick and easy shortcut, and that this shortcut does not lead us to the same place to which the highway of rationality would bring us. Few of us suffer from any illusion that the summary paths taken by our intuitions and approximations would lead us to *exactly* the same point to which reason and exact calculation might have brought us. But we do delude ourselves into thinking that we are thereby brought to a neighboring area, one that is *close enough*. To scientifically unmask this delusion is not to suggest a "different" conception of rationality, or some generic defect in our judgment, but a *rational* revision of our *specific* confidence in spontaneous reasoning and its "methods."

Before concluding on this subject, allow me to show that the current cognitive revolution is a *constructive*, not a destructive, revolution. It leads us to *deepen* our rationality, not to restructure it or, worse yet, devalue it. To show how this is true, here are two representative examples of the normative theory of rationality, taken from mathematics and logic. The doctrines set out in this theory prescribe what the correct choices are and, in a given model situation, which are the most rational judgments. From this you should quickly be able to see the radical difference between the discovery of our cognitive illusions and a genuine *crisis* in rationality. They are two distinct and separate phenomena.

A group of mathematicians working on the problem of prime numbers recently noted that a truly astronomical number could be factored into the products of two "smaller" (but still very large) numbers. Thousands of hours were spent by some of the most talented mathematicians in the world, working on the most powerful computers available, to come up with this result, and *The New York Times* announced the discovery on its front page. Up to that point, no one knew whether the number *could* be split up in the product of two smaller numbers. The number could in fact have turned out to be a prime number (and therefore would have been unable to be factored). Clearly, if a mathematician had, after much reflection and many hours spent at the computer, *wrongly* concluded that this number was a prime number, she would not have been suffering from a cognitive illusion; she would have been making a perfectly rational judgment—wrong, but rational. The error would have derived from a limitation in her reasoning, not from a cognitive illusion.

Consider now the case of the product of two numbers computed mentally in 5 seconds (see Chapter 3). By taking a whole minute instead of five seconds, one could come up with the exact product in one's mind and, given more time, pencil and paper, or a calculator, one can arrive at the correct number. In this somewhat different scenario, the rule of commutation is at work, and there is no reason to believe that someone working out a series of increasing products $(2 \times 3 \times 4 \times 5 \ldots)$ would come up with a different product from someone doing so in decreasing order $(8 \times 7 \times 6 \times 5 \ldots)$. Let us now imagine two hypothetical cases. In the first we have a respondent who makes his rapid calculation and then learns that the true result is greater than 40,000 (if he doesn't believe us, we give him the means to verify that result for himself). In the second, a respondent discovers that by inverting the order of the products, the *real* result changes (the case is entirely hypothetical, due perhaps to taking psychopharmaceutic drugs or to a "fixed" calculator). The first of our respondents finds it curious and interesting that he has underestimated the real product by such a wide margin. He will retain from the experiment, and rightly so, that he has discovered something *about himself* (about the nature of his rapid calculation). The second respondent, on the other hand, would be deeply shocked. All her certainties about mathematics would collapse. She would think that she had discovered some deep and dramatic gap in the whole rational structure of her world. It is not difficult to imagine how a cynical and able mathematician-psychologist (one able, hypothetically, to create the illusion of the non-commutability of a real product) could bring such a person close to delirium.

The two cases are radically different, and we can all *see* that they are radically different. The first reaction is typical of someone who has just discovered a cognitive illusion; the second (purely hypothetical) is typical of someone who has discovered the collapse of the founding principles of rationality. Up to this point, we have seen examples of the former not the latter type. The difference is striking, but it has perhaps not been useless to underscore the point.

The Principle of Identity and the Psychology of Typicality

Two principles are at the heart of logic: One holds that each thing is identical to itself, and the other affirms that no reasonable affirmative statement can be simultaneously both true and false. When logicians have come up against abnormal cases, such as the notorious contradiction about liars (the claim "Every statement I make is a lie" is true only if it is false and false only if it is true, hence a contradiction), they have made every effort to eliminate it or explain it, to construct a more powerful form of logic. There was talk of a deep crisis in rationality, and for decades the most able minds among mathematicians and logicians sought a way out. The results obtained by thinkers such as Gottlob Frege, Bertrand Russell, Kurt Goedel, Alan Turing, Alonzo Church, and John von Neumann are legendary. This real crisis in the canon of rationality gave rise to biographies, novels, plays, and numberless theses. No one took this crisis in traditional logic and the classical theory of sets to be a cognitive illusion; it was a real, objective limit to certain "naive" theories.

Let us now take a completely different case. Elinor Rosch, Edward Smith, Douglas Medin, Daniel N. Osherson, Daniel Kahneman, Amos Tversky, Steven Pinker, and many other psychologists and cognitive scientists have studied how a normal human subject, child or adult (say upwards of four or five years old), distinguishes the degree to which two exemplars of a single class are different or alike.

Consider the class, "birds," which includes sparrows, canaries, pelicans, falcons, penguins, and so on. The subject is given a card containing (in either words or pictures) a pair of birds (such as a canary and a sparrow, or a penguin and a duck) and is asked to list them in ascending order of similarity. These cards represent the subject's *subjective* ordering of degrees of similarity. The cards show that, *according to him*, a canary is more like a sparrow than a penguin is like a duck, or a canary is more like a duck than like a pheasant, and so on. There are mathematical procedures for manipulating these intuitive reactions, and precise scales of similarity can be built up.

The responses are dictated by a form of unconscious breaking down of the "concept" of a sparrow, a penguin, a pelican, and so on, into distinct features (but these also, through specifically designed questions, can be reconstructed in explicit fashion). In a recent experiment conducted by Osherson and his collaborators at the Massachusetts Institute of Technology, a list of 50 different species of mammals was mapped on a list of 85 characteristic features. The results showed that the instinctive response to "typicality" of a certain feature in a certain species was broadly common for most of their subjects, and varied on a continuous line from a maximum to a minimum (say from 0 to 100 percent).

If, for instance, we reconstruct the typical features of the class "birds," we base ourselves on judgments as to size, degree of domestication, beak shape, the frequency with which a given species comes into contact with humans, ability to fly, richness of plumage, the proximity of its natural geographical habitat to ourselves, the degree of friendliness it inspires in us, and so on.

Cognitive scientists have calibrated with great precision the way in which we make summary, intuitive judgments about the degree of subjective similarity between pairs of exemplars: We make a rapid, unthought-out calculation of how many and which traits the two examples have in common and how many and which features they do not have in common. Not all features carry a like "weight," they are not equally important, and we do not have an equal quantity of information for each example of the class "birds." Some features are more "diagnostic" than others, and a given feature is almost never simply present or absent, only "more or less" so (which we can express in a percentage).

Fairly sophisticated and precise mathematical models can approximate the *unconscious* mental rules we adopt to formulate these intuitive judgments of similarity. They make it possible to measure the subjective difference between any one species (such as a sparrow) and *all other species of birds.* Measuring these differences on the appropriate graphs, one can see the *average* (over the responses of hundreds of subjects) perceived difference between sparrow and canary, duck and pelican, and so on. I mean that these differences can literally be measured: on a graph, in centimeters.

The results are surprising. It turns out that we can insert— between the various object species ("birds")—another species, "birds," as though that class as a whole *were itself a specie* (rather than a set of diverse species), alongside sparrows, pelicans, canaries, penguins, and so on. Those species that appear *closest* to the anomalous "specie" ("bird") are those considered *most typical.* This spontaneous leap in our minds is a real insult to set theory and the formal theory of categories. It turns out that our minds see the whole (the class of "birds") in all its complexity *at the same level of generalization* as its discrete members, that is, particular species of birds. This is a mathematical disaster.

Children and adults see nothing wrong, for instance, in claiming that the canary is more "bird" than a penguin. Mind you, they all know that the penguin *is* a bird; there's no doubt about that, and no need to consult an ornithologist to check it out. But for all of us, the canary is a *better* example of the "bird" class than a penguin. The sparrow is more "bird" than the toucan, and so on.

The same is true of many other classes. An apple is more "fruit" than a coconut, a truck is more "vehicle" than an elevator, a lettuce is more of a "vegetable" than a radish, the Mona Lisa is more "work of art" than the Eiffel tower, the mouse more "mammal" than the hippopotamus, and so on. Lila and Henry Gleitman and their group at the University of Pennsylvania in Philadelphia have established that "7" is a better "odd number" than, say, "51" and that "4" is a more typical (hence better) even number than, say, "196." And this response is true even of those who know perfectly well what the mathematical definition of odd and even numbers is.

More recent experiments by the French cognitive scientists Jacques Mehler and Stanislas Dehaene, and by others, have shown even more conclusively that there are strong typicality effects in the world of our "mental numbers." The uniform, infinite straight line of what mathematicians call real numbers is punctuated, in our spontaneous mental representation, by very few heavy marks and signposts. Certain numbers are, to us, definitely more "typical" than others. Cognitively speaking, it is not by chance that banknotes the world over have the denominations they have (1, 5, 10, 100, etc.) and not 350 or 850, or that small change is always one-half or one-fourth of the unit currency rather than, say, one-ninth or three-sevenths. We also, for example, are more inclined to write in full letters *one thousand* than, say, *sixty-three,* though the latter word is shorter than the former.

Moreover, there are certain telescopic effects: Certain numbers appear to us mentally much "nearer" than others, and certain other numbers appear as "partly covered" by their nearest neighbors. One consequence is that the likelihood of encountering the numbers one, two, or three, in *any* text, or in a conversation, is much higher than the *cumulative* probability of encountering any of the numbers from four to nine (of course both included). This applies equally well to digits (such as *6*) and to fully spelled out numerals (such as *six*). No sheer statistical, or number-theoretical, law can explain this fact. It relies entirely upon cognitive factors of typicality and ease of representation.

Another consequence of our mental arithmetic telescopes (or tunnels, in my terminology) is that, strangely enough, if we are given a certain fixed reference number, such as 57, the time it will take to judge whether a certain other number is greater or smaller than this number decreases smoothly as we depart from the reference. It will take more time for us to "see" that 59 is greater than 57 and less time to "see" that 81 is greater than 57. The perfect smoothness in the progressive decrease of the reaction time falsifies the naive hypothesis that in carrying out such a task there ought to be a steep "barrier" right at 50, and another right at 60. The fact is that, in such a task, we do not mentally "see" the numbers as neatly partitioned into groups of "tens" and then quickly judge their relative magnitudes by paying attention to the leftmost digit. We see them as clustering densely around the reference, in a sort of mutual "occlusion" relationship. In our example, we focus on 57 and look at all the greater (respectively smaller) numbers as though they were "partly occluded" by it. To the pure mathematician, our spontaneous arithmetic must seem strange indeed.

In sum, there is no way we can "explain away" the results obtained by the Gleitmans and collaborators on the special typicality of selected even and odd numbers, such as by appealing to the fact that, say, 82 has two digits, whereas 4 has only one. Nor was it the case that their subjects could have misunderstood a question about "which one is more typical" for a question about "which one is most frequently encountered." The protocols of the experiments carefully ruled out this possibility. In fact, one can also just ask a subject to press a button as fast as he can as soon as he sees an even (or, in a similar experiment, an odd) number on the screen, interspersed among other objects, letters, and forms. By measuring the average response latencies for the same subject, one ascertains that 4 "wins" hands down in the case of even numbers, and 7 in the case of odd numbers. After all, do we not share the intimate unavowable feeling that 4 *is* a very typical even number, and that 7 *is* a very typical odd number? In fact, this is exactly what these subjects did confess, once discreetly prompted, proving that this is a very common kind of mental-numerical "feeling." Just as our rapid multiplication was susceptible to the "anchoring" effect, despite our knowing the laws of commutation, we are subject to the "prototype" of even and odd numbers, though we know the proper mathematical definition of each.

Besides these experiments with cards, other tests are possible. One can, for instance, ask each subject explicitly what is most typical of a given class; one can show schematic or realistic drawings on a screen and ask the subject to push a button the moment she sees a bird (or a vehicle, a work of art, or an even number). This latter test can be performed using very brief flashes, alternating "typical" exemplars, untypical exemplars, and some nonexemplars, or by showing pictures that contain complex scenes and many heterogeneous objects. It has been repeatedly and consistently shown that "recognition" reactions are most rapid when the scene contains the most typical exemplars of the class. This is also true for even the briefest (almost subliminal) flashes, with reactions coming within a few fractions of a second.

All these experiments agree in showing the robust *psychological reality of the typicality of a single exemplar of a given class* (birds, vegetables, vehicles, mammals, etc.). The typicality of an exemplar is then routinely measured by the *distance* between the exemplar and the class as a whole (distance between canary and bird, penguin and bird, etc.). This experiment has been performed with the most varied natural categories (birds, mammals, vegetables, fruit), with artifacts (vehicles, furniture, etc.), and with social categories (works of art, "uncle," museum, prison, island, nation, etc.).

For instance, children wholeheartedly label as an "uncle" a middle-aged man who is explicitly described to them as being neither a brother of Daddy nor of Mummy, pays frequent visits to the family, regularly takes the kids out to the zoo and to the movies, offers them candies, and is generally affectionate to them. They will not, by contrast, accept the label of "uncle" for a baby, explicitly described as a brother of Daddy (or Mummy), who lives in Australia and whom nobody in the family has ever met. Likewise, children identify as a "museum" a rich palace filled with statues and famous paintings to which nobody has access, except the owners. On the other hand, they will not identify as a "museum" a shabby shack in which dirty T-shirts belonging to famous movie stars and rock singers are exhibited daily and that anyone can visit by buying a ticket that costs one dollar. Adolescents and adults, of course, have quite different intuitions about these categories, called "nominal kinds." Typicality exerts a much greater power on children than on adolescents and adults. It is only later in life that true exemplars, satisfying the criteria of the abstract definition, such as the baby "uncle" and the shabby "museum" win over nonexemplars that possess the most superficial traits of typicality for that category.

Given that the notion of typicality had already emerged loud and clear in earlier chapters, and been shown to work its way into a number of our mental tunnels, it seemed sensible to give some idea of its psychological nature. But there are surprises still to come.

Making projections from these experiments, for instance, and arriving at our intuitive concept of "similarity" step by step, without brutal leaps, it turns out that we think North Korea is *more like* China than China is like North Korea. The Rolls Royce emblem is more like the Victory at Samothrace than the famous statue is like the emblem. Likewise, a daughter is more like her mother than the mother is like the daughter, and so on. Similarity is not a symmetrical relation: A can be more similar to B than B is to A. This may be absurd, but that is the way we silently, craftily think in some corner of our minds. The results of the experiments are perfectly clear on this score.

What emerges is that a potent factor is at work here in our judgments of similarity. We could call that factor "representativeness" or "prominence." There is a suggestive *asymmetry* in the resemblance between a prominent entity (e.g., China, the Victory at Samothrace, a mother) and entities that are, respectively, less prominent (e.g., North Korea, the Rolls Royce emblem, a daughter). This "prominence" effect has as its special case those entities *about which we know more* vis-à-vis other entities that we find alike, but about which we know less. We therefore have to distinguish between a similarity deriving "from" and a similarity "to." There is a direction in similarity judgments and there are "one-way" similarity tunnels. Although very real psychologically, this subjective similarity is *not* captured by any elegant, rational, mathematical model. The similarity judged from a prominent entity to a less prominent entity is less than the similarity measured in the opposite direction.

In terms of rationality, this is a strange and paradoxical result, but there is no doubt at all about its existence as a subjective psychological reality and its applicability to many areas of thought. Similarity, as an abstract concept, supplies us with the corresponding idea of symmetry; but for us, apparently, similarity can be asymmetrical.

Further, our subjective similarity is not even transitive. We find A is quite like B, and B is quite like C, but A is not "at all" like C. Everything lies in that *at all.* Obviously resemblances down a line will weaken, but it is not at all obvious that they should disappear, while still remaining clearly valid between A and B and B and C. Here is an easy example from before recent political upheavals. Back then, an experiment concluded that many people thought that Cuba was quite similar to Jamaica and that Cuba was quite similar to the Soviet Union; the same people held that Jamaica and the Soviet Union were in all respects very *different* from one another.

This may seem obvious, but it does make it very difficult for us to construct simple models of subjective similarity in our mental space. If similarity is *not* transitive, if it is not going to work along a line of resemblances, then the maps of subjective similarities drawn by cognitive scientists may have measurable "distances," but they can't be added up or "triangulated." Our subjective, intuitive sense of how one thing is like another has a twisted topology; its geometry is certainly not Euclidian!

Nor can our notions of typicality be assembled and disassembled according to the classical and universal rules of conjunction and disjunction, the very rules that hold true for set theory in mathematics. That hunting dog that is "more" (or "most") hunting dog does *not* derive from the "most dog dog" and the "most hunting hunting." Despite the fact that it is these two sets that create the conjunction "hunting dog," the heart of the conjunction (or union set) "hunting dog" is not derived from the conjunction of tits two respective centers (in each), or from the "center of gravity" of the two categories combined, such as "dog" and "hunting." The "most" Chinese statuette is not obtained by mentally combining the "most" typical generic statuette with the "most" typical generic Chinese artifact. The "most" pet fish is a guppy, but a guppy is a rather poor exemplar of a fish and a very poor exemplar of a pet. An excellent kitchen utensil such as a curved chopping knife is a poor instance of a utensil in general, and likewise a poor example of the generic kind of object typically found in a kitchen. An excellent example of the conjunction "chestnut dog," such as an Irish setter, is a poor instance of a generic dog and an even worse one of something generically chestnut.

For these reasons (and for other technical reasons that need not detain us here), the categories of likeness that we think about and talk about spontaneously are neither "sets" in the traditional mathematical sense nor even "fuzzy sets," those fluid sets to which individual members or subsets "more or less" belong and to which one can assign a value for their "belonging" from 0 to 100 percent. A large number of psychologically *natural* categories (birds, dogs, mammals, furniture, vehicles, islands, etc.) cluster about a prototype and have rather special properties that continue to be the subject of numerous studies and experiments.

The oddest thing of all—indeed, positively paradoxical— is that psychologically a category may not *be always like unto itself.* Here, too, progressive experiments are called for; they have to be planned with intelligence, for if the question were put to him with brutal directness, no respondent would be likely to admit that he could fall into such a logical paradox. But Tversky has shown that our minds intuitively consider some categories (those about which we know more, such as the nations of Europe) *more like themselves* than other categories (those about which we know less, such as the nations of Africa). According to Tversky, this peculiarity extends down to the single components of these categories. That is, experiments can show that there is a corner of our minds in which intuitively we think the United States is more identical to itself than, say, Brunei.

In rough outline, this is done by assembling into an inexorably logical scheme the consequences of several pieces of similarity judgments. The "trick" consists in closing a similarity "loop" in a subjective similarity chart. We start from, say, Brunei, and we move on to the next "most" similar nation, and then to the next, passing "through" the United States. In the other case, we start from the United States and then eventually return to it, after having been "through" Brunei. Given that a similarity "from" differs from a similarity "to," it turns out that when we return to our starting point, in some instances the object has *gained* in similitude (in other words, our object is now more similar to itself), whereas in other cases it has *lost* in similitude (the object is now less like itself).

These implicit judgments (made explicit in experimental conditions) are so obviously paradoxical that not all cognitive scientists are persuaded of their psychological reality. The most recent studies show some (such as Osherson, Smith, Shafir, and Stob) who admit that symmetry and identity may not be retained for whole categories but argue that these will obtain for the single objects within those categories, whereas others (such as the psychologist Gerd Gigerenzer) object to Tversky's argument even in regard to whole categories. The debate is in full flow, and it would take too long to go into all the arguments. My purpose was only to show the complex nature of the

problems we face when we seek to "map" our daily, spontaneous, intuitive judgments with logical principles, even of the
most fundamental sort (such as the identity of a thing to itself).

Let us now return to the liar's paradox. It is perfectly clear
that there is a vast difference between discovering a true logical paradox and discovering a cognitive illusion (such as makes
the United States more like the United States than Brunei
is like Brunei, or mammals more like themselves than coel-
enterata are like themselves). The liar's paradox is an objective, universal discovery concerning the structure of a formal-
ized language. An intelligent Martian, or a computer operating
according to the postulates of logic, will necessarily discover that the statement "This statement is false" is true only
if it is false and false only if it is true. The liar's paradox is necessarily a paradox for any and all intelligent beings who
can manipulate certain abstract objects by means of a certain
type of formal language. But the identity paradox, which is
implicit in our intuitive judgment of similarities and typicality,
is a paradox only to us; it is a "provincial" feature of the human
species. A Martian would probably be highly surprised to find
that we evaluate similarity in this way. The Martian's discovery
would be an empirical one about a curious species known as
Homo sapiens; it would not be a discovery about the limits of
rationality.

We can conclude that our "private" identity paradox
(which makes better known and more "typical" objects more
identical to themselves and the lesser known and less "typical,"
less identical) is no sign of a crisis in our rational world. What
is put into question is whether normative rationality, and especially classical logic, is a realistic *model* for our actual judgments. It casts doubt on the psychological hypothesis that we
are "naturally" rational beings. It does not affect the epistemo-
logical and ethical hypothesis that we should always seek to be
guided by reason. With some embarrassment we discover in
ourselves this psychological propensity for a similarity relation
that is nonsymmetrical and nontransitive. This embarrassment
is a clear indication that between our savage thinking and the

normative concepts of reason, we know we should always choose the latter.

The universal principles of logic, arithmetic, and probability calculus serve the same purpose in our cognitive illusions as the principles of optics, geometry, astronomy, and classical physics do in perceptual illusions: They tell us what we *should* see or think, not what we in fact think and see. If our intuition does in fact lead us to results incompatible with logic, we conclude that our intuition is at fault, not that logic is awry. In this sense, cognitive illusions are more like perceptual illusions than they are like true logical paradoxes.

C H A P T E R   1 0

A (Rationally) Optimistic Conclusion

We should not, just because of what cognitive science has uncovered, conclude that humankind is fundamentally irrational. Instead, we should realize that rationality is an ideal of considerable complexity, one to which we *naturally* tend, but as a sort of borderline case. The norms for choice, judgment, and rational behavior do not spring forth as a simple extension of our spontaneous psychological norms, those that dictate our actual choices. Our spontaneous psyche is not a kind of "little" or lesser reason, nor is it an approximate form of rationality. Nor, to be symmetrical, is ideal reason no more than a sort of "purified" spontaneous psychology. On specific subjects, and in specific situations, the ways of rationality and the paths taken by our mental tunnels diverge radically.

That, however, is *not* a reason to conclude, pessimistically, that our spontaneous judgments and our ideally rational judgments are always and necessarily "in conflict." They are sometimes in conflict and sometimes in agreement. The central message here is that when they are in conflict, we do not always realize that such is the case. Full-blown, self-checking rationality is not a primary, congenital given; it does not act in us spontaneously or without effort. Rational judgment brings many different forces into play, and some of them are in conflict with each other. Rationality is not, therefore, even an immediate, psychological given; it is a complex exercise that is first won, and then maintained, at a certain psychological *cost.*

The lesson we should draw from this brief exploration of our mental tunnels is that cognitive illusions are just that—illusions. And the rational ideal is just that—an ideal. The real (and not just psychological) cost of yielding to our cognitive illusions is *far greater* than the cost of triumphing over them.

Seeing no more than that indicates that Mother Nature provided us with the wherewithal to create a rational world, and to understand that we should be guided thereby if we wish to *become* rational beings. Rationality is not just "a" faculty we possess; it is not a spontaneous characteristic of our species. What is proper to our species is our capacity to discover, on our own, certain striking internal contradictions and to refute them. It is also part of our capacity as humans that we possess the basic elements from which we can construct and refine rational thought. Thus, from what we have been exploring here there is nothing to lead us to either pessimism or optimism. Using our reason means being straightforwardly realistic. We seek to recognize our limits, to understand the geography of our minds, to elaborate normative theories of rationality, and to improve our judgments—in the light of these theories, and employing a better awareness of our natural limitations.

A Super-Tunnel

I have several times referred to mental tunnels in which even the finest and best-trained minds get trapped. The kinds of tunnels into which people of this sort get trapped may be somewhat complex in their formulation, but they are nonetheless of the same *type* as those we have seen earlier. But there is one little problem left—more of a game, really—of a different kind, which is extremely easy to formulate. It has surfaced lately in the press and television, and is known as the Monty Hall problem (or paradox) after the presenter of the well-known television show *Let's Make a Deal.* Its story is well known.

Martin Gardner, the justly celebrated author of mathematical puzzles in *Scientific American* and elsewhere gave a first version of this problem in 1959. It was then called the three prisoners dilemma, and Gardner called it (not without reason, as we shall see) a "wonderfully confusing" game. An even more wonderful version, and even more confusing, was published in 1976 in the specialized magazine the *American Statistician.* I stumbled onto it for the first time in the fall of 1989, when a colleague at MIT, Daniel N. Osherson, gave a lecture on the same problem and left his audience dumbfounded. The subsequent history of this problem is no different: Wherever it is published or written about, it draws a huge, and often hostile, response. Here it is, for your own amusement and edification.

The Three-Box Game, or the Monty Hall Paradox

Though there are a number of different variations, I offer here the one I find most easy to visualize.

> On a table are three identical boxes, each with a lid, and also a neat pile of ten-dollar bills. This game is to be repeated a great many times (150, 300, 500 times, it doesn't matter, though the one running the game has to be able to afford it!). Let's say I am the one running the game.
>
> Here are the rules for each game, and every game proceeds in identical fashion. First, you leave the room, and while you are out, I put a ten-dollar bill in one of the three boxes. I then close the boxes. I know in which box the money is, but you don't. Now I invite you back into the room and you try to guess which box contains the ten-dollar bill. If you guess correctly, you win ten dollars.
>
> Each game is divided into two distinct phases. In the first, by doing no more than pointing (you are not to touch, weigh, or in any way inspect or manipulate any of the three boxes), you indicate your irrevocable choice among the three boxes, which remain closed.
>
> As you have made your choice, I open another box, one of the two remaining boxes. That box will always be an empty box—remember that I know in which box the ten-dollar bill is. (This means that if you have, without knowing it, chosen an empty box, I will open the other empty box. If, on the other hand, you have unknowingly chosen the right box, I will open either one of the other two boxes.) Having seen one empty box (the one I just opened) you now face two closed boxes, one of which must contain the ten-dollar bill.

Now comes the second phase. I now offer you the chance to stay with your first choice, or to switch your choice to the other closed box, the one you failed to choose the first time around.

This will be repeated countless times, and each time, if your second choice is right, you win ten dollars. You leave the room and the game starts all over again.

Now here's the problem: As a general rule, are you better off sticking to your first choice, or switching? What is the best strategy?

Think carefully, and ask your friends. Don't tell them right away that the very best minds have fallen into this trap, many of them still believing they were right when they were proven wrong!

I have come up against all sorts of responses. Some have insisted passionately that you should *always* switch choices; others have argued that you should *always* stick to your first choice; and still others hold that it doesn't matter at all, that you should now switch, now stick to your first choice. There are also those who, believe it or not—because they think it makes no difference—think they should always switch, or always stick with their first choice. When asked why, they will respond, "Because that's the way it is!" or "I'm basically conservative" or "I like change."

Here, I'll give you a piece of advice. Don't try this game with a lot of people in the room. The arguments won't end!

To put a little order into this kind of mental confusion, let me stipulate right away that if there were *really* no difference at all between sticking to your first choice or switching, if the probability of choosing the box containing the ten-dollar bill were *really* 50/50, then there would be *no* motive whatsoever for switching your choice, for sticking to it, or for adopting any other strategy you might devise, such as tossing a coin. But is the probability really 50/50? Your intuition tells you that you face two boxes, and one of them *must* contain the ten-dollar bill, though you don't know which. Therefore the probability *must* be 50/50. Wrong! The box you chose first has, and always will have, a one-third chance of being the right one. The other two, combined, have a two-thirds chance of containing the ten-dollar bill. But at the moment when I open the empty box, then the other one, *alone*, will have a two-thirds probability.

Hence you should *always* switch. Switching increases the probability from one-third to two-thirds. This runs totally contrary to our intuition, but is rationally absolutely right. The sum of the probabilities of the two closed boxes is, indeed, 1, but the two probabilities are *not* equal. One-third and two-thirds do add up to 1, just as one-half and one-half do. The big point is that the two possibilities do not *need* to be equal. In fact, owing to the way in which this game is constructed, they are *un*equal.

Given that a lot of first-rate minds angrily reject this conclusion, let's justify our switching in another way. Suppose for instance, that your original choice was the right one; then when I open my empty box, for you to switch will *certainly* (not just probably) penalize you. If, on the other hand, your first choice was of an empty box, you will *certainly* (not just probably) gain by switching. We have gained a little security. Let's now use that. How often do you think your choice will be correct (and thus *necessarily* penalized if you switch)? One in three times. And how often will you choose an empty box (and thus be *necessarily* better off switching)? Two times out of three.

That is why the best strategy is always to switch. You're going to win two out of three times. Yet I know from long experience that although this explanation is rationally convincing, many people still resist it—which goes to show that even with a clear argument, our initial intuition is hard to overcome. There are some highly intelligent people who simply do not accept this explanation. After a few seconds of hostile silence, they insist on starting all over again from the beginning. They want to go back to the point at which the other two boxes are still closed and they do not know which box contains the money. They refuse to accept everything that happened *before* that point, and everything that may happen *afterward;* they are firmly anchored in their primary, irresistible intuition, which tells them that, if there are two boxes on the table, the probability, must be 50/50 that one of them contains the money. I have even known people who refuse to accept this mini-demonstration that switching is necessary; they will not acknowledge that after the lid has been taken off, the boxes that remain have *different* probabilities of containing the money. Nonetheless, it is true: The two closed boxes now have a different probability of containing the ten-dollar bill.

This is simply human nature. When powerful emotions combine, the cognitive scientist walks about on tiptoe. Emotions are not her field of expertise, and the picture is hard enough without having emotions interfering.

To conclude, here is another, older version of the three-box game.

The Three Prisoners Dilemma

This is not to be confused with the prisoner's dilemma (Chapter 4, Tunnel 8).

> Three prisoners face death; they are to be shot at dawn. As the next day is the birthday of the ruling tyrant, the head of the prison decides to spare one of the condemned men. He knows which he will spare, but he is a sadist and therefore decides not to reveal to any of the three prisoners the name of the man to be spared; he wants to leave them in uncertainty until the very last moment. He tells the three prisoners that one of them will certainly be spared, but that's all he tells them. He tells the prison guard who the spared prisoner will be, but enjoins the guard to keep the secret at all costs.
>
> Filled with anguish, one of the condemned men (let's call him Prisoner C) tries to bribe the guard. He says, "As only one of us is going to be spared, it is clear that at least one of the other two of us is going to die. If you tell the name of one of those who is going to be shot for sure, I'll give you my gold watch. You're not giving away any secret, because it is mathe-

matically certain that at least one of the other two will be shot. Just give me the name of one of the two who is certain to be shot and I'll give you this valuable watch."

The guard thinks for a moment, and then lets himself be seduced. He is convinced that this will have no effect on anything; nothing is changed by telling Prisoner C. So he says, "Prisoner A will die." Prisoner C hands over his watch. He is happy because where before he had a one-in-three chance of being spared, he now has a 50/50 chance of being spared. The sacrifice of the watch is offset by his greater probability of surviving.

Question: Is Prisoner C's reasoning correct?

Gloss: if it was already certain that (at least) one of the other two must die, how is it possible that just knowing *which* of the other two will die will improve Prisoner C's chances of surviving? Isn't that magic? Again, I invite the reader to put down his book and think out his own answer to this enigma.

The correct reply is as follows: Prisoner C's chance of being spared is and remains one in three, but, thanks to the information provided by the guard, the probability of the remaining prisoner, Prisoner B, being spared has now risen to 66 percent, or a two-thirds probability.

Prisoner C has strayed into one of our mental tunnels; he has fallen into a probability trap. The only one who gains from his sacrifice of his gold watch is Prisoner B, who may know nothing at all about the transaction and has been sleeping in his cell. If it seems to you quite mad that Prisoner B's chances of survival have *objectively* increased, thanks to something that happened in which he took no part and of which he knows nothing, then yours is a cognitive illusion. An increased probability is *not* a sort of "fluid" that can pass in a jolt from one prisoner to another and produce a material change.

In the three-box problem, we dislike the idea that the chances of a box containing the money can augment or diminish while that box *always* remains closed, inert, and intact, without anything having been added to or taken away from it. That is the same illusion. We dislike the idea that Prisoner B's chances of survival have been increased by an event in which the beneficiary took no part, and about which he *knows nothing*. Symmetrically, we dislike the idea that the chances of Prisoner C, who has elicited and received the piece of information, have not changed at all. It is our view of what a probability is that betrays us. We think of probability not as an abstract mathematical entity but as a "thing," a "process"; to us it has real weight and body.

The reader can (I hope, at least) work out the solution to the problem as follows: Only one of the three prisoners is to be spared. Until the guard intervenes, each prisoner has the same probability of being spared. That is, each has a one-in-three chance of surviving (and a two-thirds chance of being executed the following morning). Prisoner A and Prisoner B have a *cumulative* probability of two-thirds or 66 percent. Now, a cumulative probability does not determine the individual probabilities; A and B together have a two-thirds probability that *one* of them will be spared. The moment the guard says that Prisoner A is *certain* to be executed, the whole of that cumulative probability passes to Prisoner B; by himself he now enjoys a 66 percent probability of survival. That he neither knows nor feels it is totally irrelevant.

Let's, in fact, pay attention to the piece of implicit reasoning that the *guard* has to follow. This piece of reasoning isn't specified explicitly in the statement of the problem, but it is obvious, and mandatory, even though it is left implicit. In fact, it is one of our mental tunnels here to disregard totally the strategy that the guard has to adopt in giving his answer. Here is the strategy, and its heavy, inevitable, probabilistic consequences.

If Prisoner C happens to be one of the two who will die for sure, then the guard will be *forced* to name the only other prisoner who will also die for sure—in our case, Prisoner A. Then we know *for sure* that Prisoner B is saved, regardless of the fact that he himself does not know this. How probable is it that this is the case? The obvious reply is two-thirds, or 66 percent. If, on the contrary, Prisoner C happens to be the lucky one, then the guard will indifferently name either of the other two prisoners, say, by tossing a coin. How often will *this* be the case? The equally obvious reply is one-third, or 33 percent. As a consequence of the strategy imposed on the guard by the logic of the situation, it matters not a whit to Prisoner C whether the guard names Prisoner A or Prisoner B. His chances were, and still are one-third, or 33 percent. But it matters *a lot* to Prisoner B that the guard has named Prisoner A, and not him. In fact, as we have just seen, this answer has a two-thirds, or 66 percent, chance of implying that Prisoner B will be saved.

The *objective* probability of an event involving any given individual may well be affected by another event taking place anywhere in the world, and quite without that individual knowing about it. Prisoner C thinks his chances of survival have jumped from one-third to one-half because he suffers from the same illusion we saw in the three-box problem: He believes that in any given situation about whose income he is uncertain, probability is subdivided equally and becomes 50/50. But here again, the only link that rigorous probability calculation allows is that the *sum* of two probabilities is 1, or 100 percent; probability theory does not claim that this sum is necessarily *equally* divided between the two remaining boxes, or the two un-designated prisoners.

There is an elegant reasoning that also shows the absurdity of Prisoner C's argument, and why his probability of survival cannot be improved. Suppose the guard says it is Prisoner B rather than Prisoner A who is sure to die.

This would make no difference at all to Prisoner C, because all he wants, following his strange way of thinking, is to rule out one of the other two as certainly condemned. Any one of the other two will do for him. In fact, the subjectively experienced boost in probability, from one-third to one-half, is tied for him to the certainty that now there are only two candidates left who could possibly benefit from pardon. Therefore, as it does not matter at all to him *which* prisoner is actually named by the guard, and because he knows for sure that at least one of them will die, he may as well toss a coin himself and pick one of the other two at random. In other words, he may as well *imagine* that there is a guard whom he manages to bribe. All this rigmarole might as well take place in the private chamber of his own imagination.

Thus Prisoner C can self-boost his chances from one-third to one-half. If, I say if, we assume that the line of reasoning of Prisoner C is probabilistically right, then he *has* a one-half (50 percent) chance of being saved. But then an identical piece of reasoning is open to *any* one of the three prisoners. Thus each of them would have a probability of one-half (or 50 percent) of being saved. This is, of course, a monstrosity from the point of view of the most basic probability theory: Their cumulative probabilities would add up to more than 100 percent (in fact, to 150 percent). This is a little proof per absurdum that shows that the reasoning of Prisoner C *cannot* be right.

Now do you see why Gardner was right to call this riddle "wonderfully confusing"? At this point, having, I hope, shown that there are mental tunnels or traps into which we all fall, and find it hard to acknowledge that we have fallen, I end my little manual of cognitive mental health.

APPENDIX A

Mental Tunnels: A Brief History of Discovery

That the argument dealing with "choice under uncertainty" is a vast new field can be deduced from a single objective fact: Significant contributions in this field have been made during the past 15 years in at least 500 specialized journals. Interest in this area is steadily growing, particularly in economic theory. Most of the experts in this field are at universities, but there are others who work in institutes of pure or applied research, in governments, in hospitals, and in financial institutions.

In institutions of pure research, the ones with which I am most familiar, the greatest progress has been made in the following disciplines (listed here not in order of the value of their contributions but by the number of contributions they have made and the means devoted to them): economics, psychology, cognitive science, psychosociology, decision theory, negotiation theory, cognitive ergonomics, epidemiology, epistemology, logic, mathematics, computer science, and medicine.

The major developments in the field have come from the United States and then, in order but lagging well behind, from

Israel, Great Britain, Germany, Scandinavia, and Switzerland. One French contribution, however, was of pioneering importance: the work of Maurice Allais on certain paradoxes in choice published in the early 1950s and very belatedly recognized by a Nobel Prize in economics. That honorable exception apart, neither France nor Italy has made substantial contributions, nor has the concept acquired much currency beyond the occasional researcher working in academic isolation.

Of all the labels that have been applied to this field, the most adequate in my view is "judgment under uncertainty," or, more exactly, "the theory and practice of decision under uncertain situations." Other labels in use (all of them including "the theory and practice of") are bounded rationality, natural rationality (as distinct from ideal or normative rationality), effective utility (as distinct from normative or expected), choice in complex situations, natural induction, and behavioral decision theory. As you can see, each of these takes up some important aspect of the subject and reflects the problem analyzed by a specific subgroup; each also reflects a certain local tradition and the history of the field.

The backdrop to all this, against which the novelty and importance of the discoveries made show up, is the classical, normative theory of rationality. This classical theory tells us how we *should* decide in uncertain situations, and what are the *best possible* rules to be used in deciding. To tell the truth, the founding fathers of this classical theory have never gone so far as to say that these theoretical norms *effectively* correspond to those in fact adopted by individuals. Mathematical probability calculus, the principles of deductive logic, the laws of economics, the theory of games, and the maximization of expected utility (this last set forth at the end of the 1940s by von Neumann and Morgenstern, and subsequently developed by Leonard J. Savage, Howard Raiffa, Duncan R. Luce, and many others), as well as the scientific rules of the inductive method, were always proposed as an ideal: that which a normally intelligent and balanced individual would *tend* to use in arriving at her judgments when she, so to speak, *did her very best*. An endless philosophical literature on the foundations of logic, economic theory, experimental science, and probability calculus deals at length with this problem. But I want to show how, since the middle 1950s, the emergence of new data and fresh hypotheses has actually revolutionized *the very way in which the problem is stated*.

The seeds of doubt about this "ideal" and the legitimacy of classical theory were sown when it began to be seen that the supposedly rational subjects—those who would react rationally to decision making—were in fact not only quantitatively but also *qualitatively* different from real subjects. What brought this home in striking fashion was the massive development of computational equipment in the decision-making process. A single famous example makes this plain.

In 1957, L. B. Lusted, a clinical researcher at the National Institute of Health, and R. S. Ledley, a dentist at the National Bureau of Standards, sought to automate on computers, and thus improve, the decision-making process by which doctors, with clinical data at their disposal, made their diagnoses. Their approach was about as classical as you could find. They based themselves on classical logic in the strictest of ways (that is, on the so-called tables of logical functions, such as negation, conjunction, disjunction, and the conditional "if . . . then") and on a hierarchy of hypotheses and subhypotheses depicted in flow charts, the arrows or "directions" of which logically linked, in a connected graph of increasing details, the probabilistically weighted hypotheses. They almost immediately realized that these automated diagnoses of theirs gave rather different results from those that the *best* clinicians might have made from the same data fed to the computer. The discrepancy between real subjects and ideal subjects in this classical case of "judgment under uncertainty" emerged with dramatic force. The dilemma that surfaced was whether it would be *more rational* to follow the conclusions of the best clinical minds or those of the computer.

A few years earlier, in 1954, the University of Minnesota psychologist Paul E. Meehl had published an explosive article, "Clinical versus Statistical Prediction: A Theoretical Analysis and a Review of the Evidence." Meehl's thesis was that statistical prediction was *more* reliable than intuitive prediction, even that of the best doctors. According to Meehl's data (which were based on an impressive body of research), the results of psychological tests analyzed by the computer were better able to predict outcomes (e.g., who might give up his studies or quit college, who might make a good pilot, who might fall back into crime, who might attempt suicide) than the personal judgments of eminent professional psychologists.

Pandemonium ensued, and a few years later Lusted and Ledley's diagnostic machine made matters even worse. Other psychologists, such as Robert R. Holt, argued against Meehl's conclusions (obviously not his data, which were beyond dispute) and recommended that data collection be improved and professional intuition be "re-educated." Two basic and different options surfaced:

1. Improve the formal apparatus (the programs fed into the computer, mathematical probability theory, logical calculus) and always choose on the basis of an *ideal* rationality.

2. Improve our intuitions, make human professional judgment more accurate, and always prefer human judgment (*aided* by normative theory and well-programmed computers).

Unable to prove that one solution was always and intrinsically superior to the other, research began on both fronts, but confidence in classical theory remained greatly undermined. Even the backers of normative rationality now felt they had to justify their choice of that method. What had always been taken for granted and as obvious now became a matter of a choice between methodologies (or even ideologies), but nonetheless *a decision itself made under uncertainty.*

A few significant articles from the preceding decades were rediscovered, such as the work done in the 1940s on "magical thinking" by Burrhus Frederick Skinner (one of the founding fathers of behaviorism, and thus of a school of thought that today seems remote from, and antithetical to, modern cognitive science). A pigeon who is fed *only* when he performs a task in his cage, but is fed *whatever* task he performs, develops highly extravagant hypotheses: For instance, he will keep turning round and round, or he will peck only in one part of his cage, or he will excrete only in one corner. Because *whatever* he does will be reinforced (by food), any "hypothesis" the pigeon develops will become fixed and stable. It then becomes almost impossible to decondition him, to shift his hypothesis to an altogether different type (note the word *type*) of behavior.

This research of Skinner's (a kind very different from that of cognitive science) was adapted to research deriving from quite different ideological bases and in very different contexts, such as that of the social psychologist and educator T. M. Newcomb. As far back as 1929, Newcomb had demonstrated examples of "magical thinking" in a group of teachers working with "difficult" children in a summer camp. The teachers were asked to keep a daily record of the behavior of 51 children suffering from various psychological problems. Newcomb's data showed that, two months later, the teachers' recollections did not concord with what they had written in their daily records (data that had been handed over to Newcomb as soon as the summer was over). A boy who'd been earmarked as aggressive or overbearing was remembered *only* for episodes in which he refused to collaborate. The *effective* frequency of these refusals, registered daily, did not in fact agree with what the teachers recalled. The average coefficient of actual behavior, as noted in the records, and that remembered two months later was a mere 27 percent. Newcomb duly noted that, on the other hand, the correlation between the boy's psychological profile and the behavior *remembered* by the teachers was at an 85 percent level.

To give some idea of how rediscoveries of old psychological literature influenced contemporary research, let me point
to the fascinating and systematic research on "preconceptions"
and "illusory correlations" (called "magic thinking" in the
wake of Skinner) by L. J. Chapman and J. P. Chapman in 1967
and then by R. A. Schweder in 1977. The psychological profiles
(of both "normal" and "pathological" subjects) of a group of
boys and girls were taken from their files and *casually* coupled
with drawings made by another boy or girl from the same
group. Next, psychology students were asked to provide justifications for the links between drawings and profiles; they were
not told that these had been put together casually. It will come
as no surprise to learn that nearly every student managed to
come up with complex and elaborate justifications. Their faith
in their own diagnostic "skill" was such that when they were
told how the drawings and profiles had been linked, they continued to justify their answers "in principle."

Ross and Lepper gave a like "magical thinking" test by asking a number of adult subjects to link real letters written by
adolescents with certain standard or ideal personality profiles,
and then to justify their linking. They divided their experimental subjects *at random* into three groups, A, B, and C, and as
each group's subjects formulated their justifications for their
"diagnostic correlation," they were assigned to either A
(encouraging), B (discouraging), or C (half encouraging and
half discouraging). That is to say those who fell *at random* into
A were told, "Good, you're making excellent correlations"; subjects in B were told, "No, that's not it at all. Think again"; and C
subjects were told now this and now that, and neither overly
praised nor overly criticized. The extraordinary thing about
this experiment, its "magical thinking," is that in each group
the respondents *continued* to consider themselves respectively
good, bad, or ordinary diagnosticians even *after* they had been
told that the praise or blame they received had been determined by their random allocation into one of the three
groups.

In the second half of the 1970s and the early 1980s came a mass of similar results. What is important here is to emphasize that this intuitive "diagnostic" judgment differs *completely* from the ideal norms of classic rationality, and that if we are to approximate (note I say "approximate" not "reach") an ideal rationality, it is *not enough* that we are informed about our illusions and the spontaneous magic of our thinking.

Even in a very brief historical overview, mention should also be made of the decisive and (on these matters) converging contribution made by two other areas of research: true cognitive science and a certain line in the development of artificial intelligence. The former, starting in the mid-1960s and increasingly in recent years, has shown that the deep divergence between real subjects and ideal subjects has its roots in our cognitive *development*. The seeds of our real and interlinked rationality are already present in the child.

In the mid-1950s, first at Oxford and then at Harvard, the noted U.S. psychologist Jerome Bruner showed that there are abstract concepts (such as the "disjunctive" hypotheses—that an object belongs to class A if and only if it is red or square and to B if and only if it is blue or circular) that are difficult to formulate or manipulate mentally. In real life, none of us *ever* spontaneously formulates a disjunctive hypothesis. If, as in Bruner's experiment, we are shown a series of cards with circles, triangles, squares, and so on of different colors, and if we are told *explicitly* and repeatedly which exemplify the concept and which don't, we formulate all sorts of hypotheses (triangular and red, circular and blue, etc.) but never do we come up with a disjunctive hypothesis (e.g., red *or* triangular). From the vantage point of formal logic there is no explanation for this, for disjunction (currently described in such formulas as "either this or that, but not both") is a perfectly decent logical function and there is a simple and coherent formal theory for deductions based on disjunctive classes. Further, as has been well demonstrated by the Harvard logician and philosopher Nelson Goodman in his classic *Fact, Fiction and Forecast, any* hypothesis may, *at any time*, be formulated in disjunctive language, and *any* set may at any time be redefined in terms of some disjunctive properties (see also Chapter 4, Tunnel 8).

The natural but alogical horror our intuition feels when faced with disjunctive hypotheses has no normative justification, that is, no rational basis. A Martian would look at our horror with amazement! Contrary to the thesis advanced by the great Geneva psychologist Jean Piaget and his school, there is also no such thing as a series of progressive, "horizontal" stage transitions from an infantile "magical" thought to "prelogical" thought and finally to a "logical-formal" adult. *Exactly* the same cognitive strategies and intuitive errors are found in adults as in children. The way in which propositions are stated and the level of difficulty of the problems are naturally different, but the strategies and mistakes are exactly alike.

If you show a child under five sets of photographs of boys and girls, but all of them with more boys than girls, he will say there are "more boys than children." Analogous experiments with selected photos of drawings show that the same children will say that there are more roses than flowers, more spoons than pieces of cutlery, and more chairs than pieces of furniture.

Past a certain age, however, the child will no longer make these "mistakes." It is not, as Piaget argued, that the very young child lacks the concept of "set" and "subset," or that older children or adults in some way develop these concepts in their heads. The case (see Chapter 2) of words ending in "ing" and words that have an "i" as their third-from-last letter is valid at any age, and proves that this is *not* a question of "possessing" the concept of sets versus subsets, but of our capacity to represent to ourselves with some facility "typical members" of a given set. The very young child finds it difficult to "see" the set of "children" (which can be either boys *or* girls—note the hatred of disjunction) in her mind; no more can she distinguish "cutlery" (which includes knives, forks, *or* spoons) and so on. We invariably think, at *whatever* age, that there are more of those groups or objects (or persons) *for which it is easier for us to represent typical examples.* Piaget's constructivist psychology, and much of development psychology in general, had already come up against cognitive illusions, but hadn't identified them as such. Their theories had come up with a way of identifying and explaining many such phenomena as proper to the childish mind; today we know they are proper to the human mind at any age. All that's needed is to follow them through into adulthood with appropriate experiments, as I have done with the various "tunnels." The arrival on the scene of the cognitive sciences has radically changed the roots of the question.

In the past few years, the cognitive sciences have also shown that many frequent and typical errors of judgment under uncertainty are part of more general and widespread errors that crop up even in *certainty* situations. In the world of artificial intelligence, starting with the pioneering work of Herbert Simon, Alan Newell, and A. D. De Groot (from 1955 on, and principally at the Carnegie Mellon University in Pittsburgh), it was soon realized that the classical probability paradigm and the laws of logic often produced insurmountable difficulties for computers. Further, problem solving and problems connected with the automatizing of induction and with generalizations made from a database showed an insurmountable *qualitative* gap between novices and experts. The novice— whether a child, an uninformed respondent, or a machine—is not a good "base" from which to start building expert knowledge. To train an expert one needs to start from scratch and develop ways and methods that are totally different, and sometimes opposite, to the ways and methods used by the novice's intuition. The novice's reasoning is often *contrary* to that of the expert. Expert judgment—as cognitive science and applied psychology in the natural sciences were also showing—does not spring from a sort of natural "prolongation" of novice judgment through generalization and abstraction. To move from novice to expert judgment requires a radical mental revolution, a deliberate radical reconstruction of the intuition.

This has been seen in detail, for instance, in elementary alge-
bra, naive physics, and naive biology—for obvious reasons the
most studied disciplines. (See Chapter 9 for a few hints of our
naive arithmetic.)

Quite independently, but in line with the other pioneering
areas, developmental psychology uncovered the fact that
throughout a child's normal development, the qualitative difference between novice and expert could be seen at every
point and in all areas of daily life (reasoning, language, problem solving, the acquisition of new concepts), and that it
worked in a highly *modular* fashion. In every area of expertise
we need constantly and specifically to reconstruct our knowledge.

The great gap between ideal rationality (that which proceeds from the rules discovered by experts and is strongly idealized) and ordinary, real judgment (that which the novice
compulsively offers) reproduces and develops its own special
angles in myriad ways. We are all novices in at least a few areas,
and choice under uncertainty is an area in which we are *always*
novices. This goes some way toward explaining why our "savage" intuitions are not only incompatible with, but also in
rebellion against the intuitive judgments of experts in statistics
and analytic method.

The only truly powerful artificial model of choice under
uncertainty turned out to be the automated chess player, but
the reasons the chess model was successful were to be found in
those characteristics that are hardly ever reproduced in real
decision making, such as simple, fixed rules and the foreseeable logic by which one's opponent moves—in fact, that the
logic of one's adversary was never completely foreseeable is
why great chess champions are still human beings, and not
machines. Over the years, at MIT, the "perceptron" developed
by Marvin Minsky, Seymour Papert, and Arthur Rosenblatt was
able to demonstrate that disjunctive hypotheses were *as* inaccessible to machines as to our own minds.

In our time, this gap between ideal and real rationality has
continued to widen. Recent paradoxes and contradictions

have appeared in feeding a machine *combined* specifications. These had always seemed perfectly compatible with each other, or even *complementary*, such as the convergence between a correct solution and the adoption of formal inductive rules, such as Bayesian probability. When it is necessary to *choose* between these specifications (showing that if a computer satisfies one specification, it *cannot* satisfy another), then the normative, classical model collapses.

There are cases being studied today in which the analyst must choose between two mutually exclusive specifications, one of which was until now considered a *logical consequence* of the other. We will not go into these by-paths, up which one discovers a highly refined theory of machines and an equally abstract new theory of rationality and inductive logic. One need only point the reader to the highly successful, but also highly technical, work published by Daniel N. Osherson, Clark Glymour, Kevin Kelly, Scott Weinstein, and Michael Stob, much of which tends to indicate that we also may be reaching a critical point in the normative theory of an ideal rationality—a subject for another book.

Why Cognitive Illusions Are Here to Stay: A Reply to Recent Critiques

T his book would have been not only incomplete but also not entirely up-to-date if it did not take into account recent attacks against the whole "cognitive illusions" approach. This attack is mainly associated with the German cognitive psychologist and historian of probability theory, Gerd Gigerenzer (see Chapter 4, Tunnel 3) Gigerenzer's work is part of a new trend, which I label—for reasons I make clear shortly—"cognitive ecology." It questions not only certain methodological details of the "cognitive illusion" approach, but also the very spirit of previous research in this field.

If the cognitive ecologists, and other psychologists who have recently embraced this new line, were right, then the message of this book would have to be drastically downplayed. In the words of the psychologist Lola L. Lopez, this whole field, and a book such as this one in particular, would consist of nothing but "rhetoric." Nay, as she entitled a particularly nasty 1991 critical article, we would all be guilty of "the rhetoric of irrationality." Gigerenzer and collaborators always pay due formal respect to the pioneering discoveries of Tversky and Kahneman, yet these authors claim to have opened a new horizon "beyond heuristics and biases." They do not hesitate to label the kind of research set out in this book "a cul-de-sac," a "conceptual dead-end."

In some corners of our profession, the ecologists have occasionally managed to create an atmosphere hostile to the notion that we all are—at least at times, and at least when faced with certain specific problems—spontaneously irrational. Reduced to its essence, and backed by specific new data, their argument is that our mental setup, if properly understood, is, *where it really matters,* basically fully adequate to deal with the problems of everyday life. According to these authors, many of the mental tunnels we have met with here are produced by weird and unnatural problems, by contrived and exceptional setups, by plain linguistic misunderstanding on the part of the subjects, and by methodological errors. Gigerenzer argues that, "Despite its influence, the 'heuristics and biases' program is merely an important transitional stage, which must be transformed if long-term progress is to be made."

I do not intend here, for reasons of space and because much of the argument is highly technical, to offer a full account of the theses and the data presented in this literature. Nor is this the place to make a point by point rebuttal of the cognitive ecologists' critiques. Frankly, like Tversky and Kahneman themselves, I am unimpressed by what the cognitive ecologists say. Nonetheless, for the sake of completeness, I at least attempt to sketch their approach and summarize the main reasons I think the thrust of their conclusions is wrong. A few short quotations from some of these papers, and a summary of the new experiments, should suffice to give the reader the flavor of this critique. Here are some of the main points of attack, and the characteristic logic the cognitive ecologists use to draw vast conclusions from their new, different, and "better" experiments.

Neglect of Base Rates

The sweeping conclusion of these authors is, to quote from them directly, that "It is nonsensical to talk about a neglect of base rates." Why? Let us take the engineers/lawyers case (Chapter 4, Tunnel 4).

It turns out that if subjects physically extract a profile from an urn that they know contains the profiles of 70 engineers and 30 doctors, and if they do so one by one and at random, then they do not at all neglect the proportion between the two. Evidently, it is not enough simply to tell the subject that there is a certain proportion of engineers and lawyers. The random sampling has to be made clear, vivid, and palpable. Then the neglect of base rate disappears. Moreover, if informative profiles, truly typical of engineers or lawyers, are given very early in the task, then the stated proportions are neglected because, according to Gigerenzer, the subjects are induced to assume that *all* the profiles are somehow informative. If, on the contrary, neutral profiles (such as Dick's; see Chapter 4, Tunnel 4) are offered first, then there is a markedly lesser neglect of base rates.

The explanation offered by Gigerenzer and collaborators is that stereotypical descriptions focus attention away from base rates and implicitly invite respondents to ignore the stated proportions of engineers and lawyers. Subjects are actively trapped into neglecting base rates, and quite reasonably do what they are told, though implicitly, to do. Direct visual observation that the extraction of profiles is indeed random, however, or starting off with uninformative profiles, redirects their attention to the base rates.

Now let's take the taxicab accident (see Chapter 4, Tunnel 6). The imaginary jurors are now allowed to enquire freely about the information they would like to have, in order to give their estimate of the probability that the taxicab was indeed blue. They are allowed to seek "contextually" and "ecologically" more valuable data. To cut a long story short, people spontaneously and correctly realize that it would be more informative to be told how many cabs of each color were circulating at the time of the accident that night, not in general but in the specific neighborhood the incident took place, and what proportion of taxi drivers in each company are statistically prone to accidents (even better, the past record of involvement in hit-and-run accidents for each company). When supplied with such much more accurate and more relevant information, subjects do not neglect base rates. Neglect, according to the cognitive ecologists, is induced only by the vague statement of the problem and by the "irrelevant" information offered. Free people to gather information on the case as they see fit, and there will be no neglect.

Here I would be strongly tempted to bring this line of reasoning to the extreme. Why not simply tell the jurors who the driver really was, or the cab's license number? Then we wouldn't have to deal with base rates at all. Big deal, indeed. But let's continue.

Leda Cosmides and John Tooby, in a very recent long article on the case of the clinical test (Chapter 4, Tunnel 6), claim to have seriously undermined the idea that there is a neglect of base rates in clinicians and medical students. We do not have to worry about this mental tunnel, "because" (I really do have to put this in quotation marks) if the same problem is posed to a subject in the form of a set of elaborate graphs that vividly represent—with squares, circles, red marks, and such—the percentages of (1) people who test positive but do not have the illness, (2) people who test positive and indeed do have the illness, and (3) people who test negative and do not have the illness, and so on, then (miracle, miracle) there is no neglect of base rates. Their punchline is that the *format* of the information determines whether there will be a neglect of base rates.

I leave my counter-critiques for later. Let's now have a brief look at the ecologists' critique of another tunnel.

Overconfidence

The conclusion from new experiments, in Gigerenzer's words, is: "One cannot speak of a general overconfidence bias anymore, in the sense that it relates to deficient processes of cognition or motivation. In contrast, subjects seem to be able to make fine conceptual distinctions—confidence versus frequency—of the same kind as probabilists and statisticians do."

The cognitive ecologists' new experiments separate into distinct subsets or groups simple and straightforward questions about "representative" cases (such as "Is Berlin north or south of Rome?") from "tricky" questions about nonrepresentative cases ("Is Rome north or south of New York?"). The subject's confidence is then calibrated separately for the answers to each subset of questions. Another innovation is to ask the subjects for their subjective degree of confidence, not on single answers to single questions, but on the frequency of correct answers in a subset ("How many of these 50 questions do you think you got right?").

Not surprisingly, overconfidence turns out to vary as widely as the groups vary, and it is less marked, or even absent, when subjects are asked about their *cumulative* average confidence over entire groups of questions. Moreover, if one starts by asking particularly tricky questions and then progressively inserts easier questions into the lot, then there is underconfidence. The subject, as a matter of fact, gives more correct answers than he thinks he is giving. A rather elaborate cognitive and probabilistic theory is proposed to account in detail for all these findings.

The new theory is, in Gigerenzer's words, "based on the more charitable assumption that people are good judges of the reliability of their knowledge, provided that the knowledge is representatively sampled from a specified reference class." In other words, only if you select tricky questions, about unnatural "nonrepresentative" knowledge items, is there then overconfidence.

Probability Blindness

Gigerenzer is an expert on the history of statistics and probability theory. His constantly recurring claim is that Tversky and Kahneman, and all the researchers in the recent "cognitive illusions" tradition, misrepresent the normative theory. "Researchers have relied on a very narrow normative view, and have ignored conceptual distinctions—e.g., single case versus relative frequency—fundamental to probability theory. By recognizing and using these distinctions, however, we can make apparently stable 'errors' disappear, reappear, or even invert."

For instance, Gigerenzer claims that "there are other Gods besides Bayes' theorem, even statistical ones." "Statistics speaks with more than one voice," and because there are several equally valid statistical normative theories, then (again in Gigerenzer's own words), "the normative pillars of the program of Kahneman, Tversky and others collapse. Specifically, the key problem is a simplistic conception of normativeness that confounds one view about probability with the criterion for rationality." The critical point in the current context (see Chapter 4, Tunnel 4) is the following argument offered by Gigerenzer.

If one espouses a strict frequentistic interpretation of probability, Gigerenzer says, then the very idea of computing the probability of a single event has no meaning at all, and one cannot even speak of probabilistic illusions in this domain, because there is no rational standard, no rational "norm," that allows us to label them as illusions.

If, on the other hand, one espouses the subjectivist interpretation of probability (one that conceives probability, roughly, as a privately consistent, all-things-considered betting strategy), then single events do have a probability, but subjective estimates of that probability are by definition always "rational." Gigerenzer likes to quote a passage written in 1931 by Bruno de Finetti, the founding father of the subjectivist theory: "However an individual evaluates the probability of a particular event, no experience can prove him right, or wrong; nor in general, could any conceivable criterion give any objective sense to the distinction one would like to draw, here, between right and wrong." Gigerenzer's punchline then is, "Prominent thinkers can still be found in every camp, and it would be bold unto foolhardy to claim that any interpretation had a monopoly on reasonableness."

The Selection Task and Cheater Detectors

Another reason the cognitive ecologists are so determined to undermine the "heuristics and biases" findings is their total reliance on evolutionary considerations. They find it suspect that our long evolutionary history should have endowed our species with dubious, or even dangerous, cognitive reflexes. Because they endorse the idea of an evolutionary long-term adaptation to the environment, a sort of cognitive survival of the fittest, and because our having inherited cognitive illusions would make us not particularly fit for the world in which we live, the ecologists are compelled to claim either that these illusions do not exist at all or that they are not illusions.

The answer may be that we should reevaluate the real "ecological validity" of our cues, and tests, of our spontaneous reasoning and our natural intuitions. What is perhaps less useful or even useless today must surely have been useful when our species was evolving. Cognitive ecologists are in fact seeking to relocate our spontaneous mental strategies and intuitions into their proper ecology.

Occasional shortcomings revealed by contrived and overly academic tests should be reinterpreted in the light of the *correct* solutions to typical puzzles and predicaments in the world in which we evolved. This is a typical statement (again by Gigerenzer): "Cognitive functions are adaptations to a given environment . . . . [Therefore,] we have to study the structure of environments in order to infer the constraints they impose on reasoning." Leda Cosmides and John Tooby also have endorsed this approach, called "evolutionary psychology."

These are typical examples:

1. If you are at the dean's birthday party and you see a 50-year-old man with a gray beard, thick glasses, and a rumpled tweed jacket, you do not guess his profession by drawing from the base rates in a random population of males of that age. You are perfectly justified to neglect base rates and assume he is a professor. The lawyers and engineers problem is very different from real life, in which it is perfectly sensible to be guided by typicality.

2. Let's reconsider ease of representation, and Bertrand Russell's maxim (see Chapter 7, "Ease of Representation"). Nisbett and Ross have made famous a fallacy known as the Volvo fallacy.

This is the standard test. You are told that, (1) a trustworthy poll among some 10,000 current Volvo owners certifies the Volvo to be a perfectly reliable car, and (2) yesterday you saw your neighbor, a Volvo owner, stranded on the road because of an engine failure. Then, you are asked to evaluate the probability that your next car will be a Volvo.

As we all understand, and as Russell had rightly forewarned, the vivid experience of our neighbor weighs much more heavily than all those other remote 10,000 witnesses to the contrary. It may well be argued, as Nisbett and Ross do, that this is a fallacy. But Gigerenzer assaults this judgment. He claims our reaction is perfectly rational. Were we to imagine ourselves back in the jungle, and leading a most primitive, literally aboriginal, sort of existence, and if in our native village people have been swimming happily in the local river for as long as anyone can remember but yesterday your neighbor's son was eaten by a crocodile while swimming in the river, is it not then perfectly reasonable to disregard the long past record and refrain from swimming in that river?

The upshot is that ease of representation can well have its merit. It is no fallacy at all in realistic ecological settings.

3. Reconsider Wason's selection task (see Chapter 7). You will recall that the bias shown in that task was in favor of instances that confirm a given hypothesis and against instances that deny it. Logic would dictate a certain minimal choice of cards, but our own bias makes us select different cards. Gigerenzer and Hug, and Cosmides and Tooby, have bravely striven to show that this bias makes perfectly good sense in an evolutionary context. What we tend to do spontaneously is to turn up those cards that give us the best chances to detect possible cheats in what is a situation of social contract.

Briefly, the upshot of several widely publicized scientific articles on our innate "cheater detectors" is that, were we programmed spontaneously to follow the laws of logic, we would be prone to being cheated in real-life social interactions. But we are differently programmed, and rightly so. We are "natural" in violating the laws of logic here because, by so doing, we maximize our chances of unmasking potential scoundrels and free-riders in situations of social contract.

Suppose a generic social contract read, "If you pay the cost, then you may enjoy the benefits." You are presented with four cards (à la Wason and Johnson-Laird, see Chapter 7, "Magical Thinking"), and the upward faces of the cards state:

A. This is someone who has paid the cost.

B. This is someone who has not paid the cost.

C. This is someone who is enjoying the benefits.

D. This is someone who is not enjoying the benefits.

To check whether the conditional law "If . . ., then . . ." indeed applies, pure logic would impose that we turn cards A and D. But these cards are totally irrelevant for detecting possible cheaters. Who cares whether individual D has or has not paid the cost? And who cares whether A is or is not enjoying the benefits? He paid the cost anyway! Rather, in the teeth of pure logic, in order to detect possible cheaters, it is vital to turn cards B and C, which is what most of us tend to do instinctively.

Gigerenzer and Hug, and Cosmides and Tooby, have tested subjects on an impressive array of social contract situations, confirming that we indeed are naturally good cheater detectors. Once again, their take-home lesson is that in real-life cases, and most notably in situations of social contract, so vital to the evolution of our species, it is not a fallacy to violate the laws of pure logic. The spontaneous cognitive strategy of verification that our own nature dictates is exactly the one that makes most sense from an evolutionary point of view.

This brief summary of a voluminous, and fast growing, literature will have to suffice for our present purposes. Now, here are, in summary, my countercritiques.

First and foremost, one must avoid the following reduction to absurdity. Let's take the Müller-Lyer figure (Chapter 1). Obviously, if one erases from the drawing all the little "wings," then the two segments do indeed appear of equal length. It would be "bold unto foolhardy" to claim that "therefore" the Müller-Lyer figure is no optical illusion. It is senseless to deny the existence of an illusion, be it perceptual or cognitive, on the mere ground that the illusion disappears when the situation is altered, even slightly.

The discovery of genuine illusions is made difficult by the delicate and unstable complex of factors that must be precisely assembled to reveal the effect. This counter-objection accounts for the alleged disappearance of the neglect of base rates and overconfidence. It is interesting that these cognitive illusions attenuate, or even disappear, in the experimental situations I have summarized above. This in no way cancels, or reduces, the remarkable and worrisome fact that the illusions are present and vivid in other common situations we have previously tested, a fact confirmed by further experiments carried out by these very authors.

In the case of the dean's party, the central thesis advanced by the cognitive ecologists is that we have a fine natural flair for the relevant samples from which to calculate base rates, and therefore probabilities (in this case, the small subset of human beings who frequent the dean's parties). Should we spot the same guy on the stage at an Academy Awards ceremony, we would presumably guess his profession quite differently. The counter to this objection is that we have to pay attention to base rates *anyhow,* and that there is nothing particularly contrived, or irrelevant, or socially unrealistic in considering a set of engineers and/or a set of lawyers. The fact remains that spontaneous shallow judgments based on clichés (i.e., typicality) *do* win over estimates of base rates, *even* in cases that are perfectly "ecologically natural." And the fact remains that this is something disturbing that happens to us but shouldn't.

It also remains a fact that in the perfectly ordinary situations presented in this book, clinicians and jurors still do fall prey to the neglect of base rates. The "corrective" factors highlighted in these new experiments may well be useful in the design of better academic curricula, and in a more careful presentation of trial cases. They in no way refute our basic propensity to fall into these illusions. And this is a most alarming fact. I consider it socially irresponsible on the part of the cognitive ecologists to try to create an atmosphere of serenity and carelessness about the dangers of our mental tunnels.

Another *reductio ad absurdum* of the ecologists' critique can easily be built upon the dean's party, or on the case of the crocodile in the river. One cannot "prove" that there are no red objects in a room because there are also green objects in that room. The presence of green objects only refutes the thesis that all the objects in the room are red. But no one ever claimed that every projection from past experience, and every memorization of typical situations, leads to fallacies and cognitive illusions. The thesis is that they *sometimes* do, and that among the cases in which they do so there are many that prompt us to correct ourselves.

The crocodile story cannot prove that it is rational today, in our world, to value the mishap of one single neighbor more than the opposite experience of 10,000 satisfied bathers. This is an all too common and almost irresistible mental tunnel from which we should emerge at once. A former secretary of the budget has written that a powerful motivation behind Reagan's whole tax reform was his vivid recollection of a California friend who had decided to work less because his additional income would have been taken away by the Internal Revenue Service. It is methodologically objectionable to belittle the dangers of the "ease of representation" bias by offering cases in which it works well. It is even more objectionable on social and educational grounds, given the regrettable consequences to which such errors lead in our own world today.

As to the frequentistic versus subjectivist interpretations of probability, what I have to say is simple, and lethal to the cognitive ecologist position. People have quite vivid and clear intuitions about the probability of a single event. Even if that could be shown to be meaningless, as frequentists claim, this would not prevent people from continuing to entertain systematic and readily reproducible intuitions. Because these single events are usually those that most affect oneself or one's closest relatives, and because they demand serious decisions, it is very important to help us think straight in these matters.

The probabilistic illusions we have encountered are illusions—no possible doubt about that. Ordinary people learn about them with embarrassment and, once alerted, develop a healthy tendency to try to avoid them. That this is so is shown not only by the way in which proofs and rational arguments (as we have offered, for instance, with the three boxes and the three prisoners problems) generally persuade in the long run, but also by the fact that repeated questions alone, even before any explanation or proof is given (as in the case of the maternity ward), make subjects feel uneasy.

Whether this is so because of normative conceptions of rationality, or simply with a subject being "right" or "wrong," is up to a point a terminological dispute. What counts is that everyone's life would be better if we learned to correct many of these spontaneous probabilistic intuitions of ours, and there are "reasons" that we would be better off. I mean that we can argue for these improvements with chains of propositions that carry conviction (such as mini-proofs of the sort I offer in this book). Our illusions and their correction are not just "brute" facts about the vagaries of the world. To maintain that we should try correct these tendencies in ourselves whenever possible is certainly not "bold unto foolhardy." It is irresponsible to claim the contrary.

Finally, the conceptions of biological evolution that we have today, with the exception of those of a very few real specialists, are demonstrably so naive and simpleminded that it is a safe bet that one day they will be a source of considerable embarrassment. We shall all be embarrassed by our sweeping statements in the years to come. Suffice it to remind the reader that insects had evolved at least ten elaborate forms of mouthpieces, uniquely "adapted" (one would say) to their feeding upon flowers, one hundred million years *before* there were any flowers on Earth. Try to explain *that* with the notion of adaptation. Present-day evolutionary psychology and cognitive ecology are pathetic attempts to deduce from a few paleo-Darwinian adaptationist clichés certain "constraints" on the evolution of the human mind. The real process must have been, to all evidence, the most intricate and complex phenomenon with which science will ever have to grapple. As Richard Lewontin aptly reminds us, we know nothing at all about the evolution of cognition.

As I said, we shall all be embarrassed, in the fullness of time, by the naiveté of our present evolutionary arguments. But some will be vastly more embarrassed than others.

Tunnel Exits

Solution of the Three-Card Problem

The answers of the vast majority of subjects to the three questions are one-third to (1), one-half to (2), and one-half to (3). (If we prefer, respectively, 33 percent, 50 percent and 50 percent). In this case, it is overwhelmingly likely that a subject also answers one-half to (2'), and one-half to (3') (because these are perfectly symmetrical, as contraries, to (2) and (3)).

The most interesting questions, of course, are (3) and (3'). Let's take (3) (a perfectly analogous piece of reasoning also applies to (3')). A powerful intuition here is the following: Because we *know* that the drawn card has landed with a red side up, *then* we can safely exclude that the drawn card is the white-white card. Therefore, the drawn card can *only* be the red-red one *or* the white-red one. It follows that the probability that the other side is also red is one-half (50 percent). (The answer to (3') is also one-half, or 50 percent.) This powerful and cogent (but provably wrong) intuition is the signal cause of our "Dutch bookability."

Let's, in fact, consider a different piece of reasoning: There are—all in all—three red sides and three white sides. The fact that the card has landed with a red side up excludes two white ones (it *is* a fact that the white-white card is ruled out) but still leaves one white and two red sides as possibilities. Therefore, the probability of another red on the hidden side is two out of three, or two-thirds (66 percent). (The "secret" here is to count *each* side of the red-red card as one distinct possibility.) (The "symmetrical" answer to (3′) is, now, one-third, or 33 percent.)

These two pieces of reasoning, and the associated probabilistic intuitions, *once the second is explicitly offered* (as I have done here), appear to most subjects almost equally compelling. But clearly, if one is correct, then the other can't also be. We must make up our mind and choose one and only one. It can be demonstrated, on the basis of the axioms of probability theory, that the second intuition is correct, whereas the first one is incorrect.

A fully rigorous mathematical proof would strain the patience of our readers (it can be found in the 1994 paper by Osherson and in the references cited therein), but let's see approximately how it proceeds.

According to the good canons of probability calculus, if the probability that something happens is p, then the probability that that very same thing does *not* happen is $1 - p$. (If there is a 40 percent chance of rain tomorrow, the chance of "not-rain" is 60 percent.) Moreover, we have to agree on *how* to conduct a fair wager based on a "conditional," such as the ones in (3) and (3′) (*assuming* that the drawn card lands with a red side up—this is something we grant—*then*, what is the probability that the red-red card was drawn?). The standard canons are that we neither win nor lose if (in this case) the drawn card does *not* land with a red side up. Any time we see a white side facing us the stakes are simply refunded. But *if* the drawn card *does* land with the red side up, then the (3) wager is won just in case the other side is also red and lost just in case the other is not-red (that is, white). Because we are bewitched by the piece of reasoning that concludes there is a 50 percent chance that the hidden side is also red, we will accept a fair wager accordingly, such as, we win $4 if red-up and red-red, we lose $4 if red-up and *not* red-red (the other side is white), and finally (as we said), if white-up to begin with, we neither win nor lose.

Keeping these simple and coherent rules in mind, and abiding by them scrupulously, we are ready to proceed. Let's be reminded that we sincerely and firmly judge that the probability for (1) is one-third; for (2) one-half; and for (3) one-half (also (3′) will receive a rating of one-half). Therefore, let's fix the stakes accordingly:

1. Win $4.20 if red-red; lose $2.10 otherwise.
2. Win $2.00 if white-up; lose $2.00 otherwise.
3. Lose $4.00 if red-up and white-down; win $4.00 if red-up and red-down; neither win nor lose if not red-up.
3′. Win $4.00 if red-up and white-down; lose $4.00 if red-up and red-down; neither win nor lose if not red-up.

Trivially, because of the way the questions have been formulated, if one wins (3), then one loses (3′), and the converse. The introduction of (3′) just makes the little proof here below more intuitive. Okay, let's run the game.

It is easy to see that we will inevitably lose money no matter what card is drawn and no matter how it lands. We have been, indeed, Dutch booked.

SITUATION 1

Some card other than red-red is drawn, and it lands with a white side up. We lose bet (1), win bet (2), and neither lose nor win bet (3′). Overall, we lose 10 cents.

SITUATION 2

Some card other than red-red is drawn, and it lands with a red side up. We lose bet (1), lose bet (2), and win bet (3′). Overall, we lose 10 cents.

SITUATION 3

The red-red card is drawn, and it lands (you bet!) with a red side up. We win bet (1), lose bet (2), and lose bet (3'). Overall, we lose $1.80.

There is no other situation that could conceivably occur, and we have lost some money in each and every of the possible three situations that *can* occur.

It can be shown in full rigor and generality that we can avoid being Dutch-bookable, if, *and only if,* we place our bets according to the axioms of probability theory. In this particular case, if we adopt the second line of reasoning, and thereby assign to (3') a probability of one-third (and to (3) a probability of two-thirds), then no one, absolutely no one, can build a Dutch book on our probabilistic judgments. We are safe.

A little caveat: Assuming that our interlocutor can be persuaded to bet (it may be the case that he or she refuses to make *any* bets at all), then it can be argued that being (or not being) Dutch bookable in a specific problem situation (such as the three-card problem) is a hard *fact*, something that can be mathematically demonstrated to anyone's satisfaction, and then, on top of it, experimentally verified through a series of actual runs. Then the persuasiveness of an argument for the irrationality of a certain betting strategy is indeed crushing. Mathematics and dollars nicely combine to make a certain strategy, and the probabilistic intuitions behind it, *absolutely* irrational, not just in the eyes of the theoretician, but also (so to speak) in the eyes of God himself. Dutch bookability surely is a very cogent argument, but it cannot always be turned into an "absolute" argument, unless the subject can be fully and rationally *persuaded* that he is losing money *because* he is Dutch bookable. One problem is that every series of runs (be it real or simulated) must be finite, and it may prove hard to convince a "true believer" that she would not start "recovering" after a very long series of runs. We have to convince her that she is losing money *because* she has entered a Dutch book, not because she simply "happens" to be unlucky. An argument for the rationality of certain betting strategies (and of the underlying beliefs and intuitions) built on the basis of Dutch bookability must make this causal link perfectly transparent. Such an argument can sometimes, at least in the limit, prove just as cogent as (but no more than) a standard rational argument not based on Dutch bookability. In other words, Dutch bookability can only appeal as a knock-down argument to a person who accepts bets in the first place and who grants us a number of central assumptions and ideal conditions of verifiability about rationality itself. However, barring these subtle and highly technical niceties, in all the ordinary situations of decision making and real betting, it *is* irrational for anyone to insist on maintaining some intuition (and/or belief) that demonstrably leads to Dutch bookability. The three-card problem really *proves* that the first line of reasoning *is* wrong, even if it is judged intuitively very appealing by the vast majority of us.

Answer to the Syllogism Involving Ministers and Composers

The *only* correct conclusion is: *Some thieves are not composers.* Or, if you'd rather, *There are thieves who are not composers.* (In our context, the difference here is only a matter of style, not of substance.) That this is an incontestable result is to be found in the fact that it is *logically impossible* for the two premises to be true, and for this conclusion not to be true. For purists and logicians who can split a hair four ways, let me add that this conclusion is logically unassailable, so long as it is certain that in the country in question, which must be a real country, there exist the two categories, and that they be called "ministers" (or cabinet secretaries) and "composers." In fact, one has to avoid the situation in which these sets are empty. Rephrasing the premises as "all *the* ministers" and "all *the* composers" may aptly reinforce in the subjects the assumption that there are ministers and that there are composers. As the distinguished logician George Boolos of MIT has put it, the sentence "All desert-

ers will be shot" can be true also if there are, in fact, no desert-
ers. In these cognitive tests, one wants to avoid such limited
cases. For a further and accurate account of this problem, the
reader is referred to Philip Johnson-Laird's *Mental Models*,
Chapter 6, and to his exchange with George Boolos in the journal *Cognition* in 1984 (see "Suggested Reading").

Answer to the "Brief Speleology of the Mind"

First product (with increasing numbers): Taking the mathematical average of the replies received from many respondents
(students at Stanford University, at the University of British
Columbia, or at Tel Aviv University), one arrives at 512.

Second product (with decreasing numbers): The average
is 2,250.

The exact reply, as anyone can verify, is 40,320.

Tunnel 1

The average preference, as expressed by a very large sample of
respondents: 72 percent favor A and 28 percent favor B.

The average preference expressed by the second sample
of subjects tested shows a reversal of these preferences: 22 percent favor C and 78 percent favor D.

Tunnel 2

The numbers obtained by Kahneman and Tversky in a series of
actual experiments, in the first case (Tables A and B), the average is $60. It should be noted that an average recorded mini-
mum of $40 is required to compensate for an increase of $10
in the possible loss. This goes against every criterion in a
rationally calculated compensation. In the second case (Tables
C and D), the average is $52. In this case (all win, no loss) a

puny $12 more will compensate for a reduction of $10 in the prize. The whole game is now down to a $2 "compensation."

The psychological asymmetry between possible gain and possible loss is flagrant. The advantage of tests such as these is that they make it possible to measure this asymmetry with considerable accuracy. As we have seen, it amounts here to nearly 20 times. An increase of $10 in a risk of loss that has been fixed at 50 percent requires—or so says our intuitive estimate—compensation (still at the same fixed probability of 50 percent) at least four times greater. Our fear of losing easily wins out (by 20 times) over our enthusiasm for winning. These are signs of an *extreme* basic conservatism, and it should give decision makers pause. Add to this fear others, and the disequilibrium between possible wins and possible losses can only increase.

Tunnel 3

Here are the exact figures, as published by Tversky and Kahneman. If the respondent makes the following ranking

$$A < C\&J < J \text{ for Bill}$$

and ranks as follows

$$F < T\&F < T \text{ for Linda}$$

he is clearly subject to the conjunction effect. This ranking was made by 87 percent of the respondents for Bill and by 85 percent for Linda.

It is interesting to see how these cumulative percentages are split among uninformed respondents, semi-informed, and experts in statistics:

Uninformed		Semi-Informed		Expert	
Bill	Linda	Bill	Linda	Bill	Linda
89%	83%	90%	92%	85%	86%

Tunnel 5

Here are the average responses derived from a large number of subjects:

In the larger clinic	24%
In the smaller clinic	20%
No difference	56%

More than half the respondents, therefore, hold that statistical fluctuation does not depend on the size of the sample. The correct answer is "in the smaller clinic," because the smaller the clinic, the more likely the fluctuation. This is in fact amply demonstrated in the case in which *all* births are of the same sex. Even intuitively we should now be able to see that it is more likely that there might be 15 births of the same sex on the same day than that there might be 45. The tiny fraction of those subjects who answered correctly from the start face no trauma when they pass to the second case (all births of the same sex). But anyone who answered "in the larger clinic" or "no difference" (some 80 percent of the respondents) is perplexed. Maya Bar-Hillel has in fact established that when extreme fluctuations are proposed (100 percent of all births are of the same sex), more than 80 percent of the respondents give the correct answer. When in the test respondents are offered percentages rising from 60 to 100 percent as the base for "special days," the average of correct responses grows, but this growth is not linear; the curve rises rather slowly, and leaps forward only when extreme (90 percent and above) percentages are offered.

Tunnel 6

The right answer is calculated according to Bayes' law. Here I offer a greatly simplified, "intuitive" version; I put "intuitive" in quotation marks because we have seen ample evidence that these calculations are not in fact intuitive for us. The task is to *educate* our intuition, step by step, through a version of Bayes' law that conserves, to the extent possible, those few of our intuitions that are *correct*. The formula is set out with perfect rigor in many treatises on probability theory, and I refer the shrewder reader to those treatises.

Here is the technique: First one sets out a table that states the different percentages in a number between zero and one (a 25 percent probability will be written as 0.25, a 79 percent probability as 0.79, and so on). I transcribe here from data used by R. E. Snyder in a classic study from 1966 based on the effective diagnostic capability of a mammography in detecting a malignant tumor:

		Illness	
		Present	Absent
	Positive	0.79	0.1
Test			
	Negative	0.21	0.9

For simplicity's sake we have assumed that the percentage of "false positives" (those who test positive but are not ill) is the "complement" of the true negatives (those who test negative and are not affected)—in other words, their sum is 100 percent. In real life things are never quite so simple, but there is no reason to make our calculations more difficult. The true positives are those who seem, to our intuition at least, to exhaust all one needs to know about the reliability of the test. In fact, the way the test is set up, the test has already been described as 79 percent reliable. Let whoever refused to answer until she knew what the total number of false positives was cast the first stone. None of us ask about this last bit of information, thought as we now know, it is all-important. The best way of defining the top-left figure (that is, the number of true positives) is with reference to the sensitivity of the test.

The table above contains all the elements we need to apply Bayes' law save one, which in fact was explicitly provided in the text of our test: the probability of being ill *independent* of the results of the test, which is 1 percent, or 0.01. Basic to this calculation is the product of the sensitivity of the test (true positives) and the *base* probability—that is, the overall chances of a patient having the illness, whether or not she takes the test. Let's call this product WA (for weighted average). In our example, then, the result is:

$$WA = (0.79) \times (0.01) = 0.0079$$

You will note this amounts to about a 1 in 8,000 chance.

The next step under Bayes' law requires another calculation. This calculation requires us to find the product of two figures: (1) the probability of a patient *not* having the illness, though she tests positive, and (2) the probability that she doesn't have the illness quite independent of the test. In our tables, false positives number 0.1 (10 percent). The second figure is 0.99 (or 99 percent). This figure we obtain by reversing the probability of the patient having the illness independent of the test. As that was 0.01, we arrive at 0.99.

Multiplying 0.1 by 0.99 we obtain the product 0.099. We may intuit that this figure is another "weighted" probability: the probability of a pessimistic diagnostic error (due to the sensitivity of the test) multiplied by the high, optimistic probability of not having the illness, whatever the test says. Let's call this product OE, for optimistic error. Bayes' law now asks us to combine these various figures in the following manner (and our intuition is of no help here; it needs reeducation before it can "see" what this formula means).

Real probability of having the illness *given that* the test is positive:

$$\frac{WA}{WA+OE}$$

Our WA is 0.0079 and our OE is 0.099. The final probability is 0.0739, or roughly 7 percent.

The case of the taxi accident is strictly analogous.

$$WA = (0.8) \times (0.15) = 0.12$$
$$OE = (0.2) \times (0.85) = 0.17$$

The effective probability of the taxi being blue is

$$\frac{0.12}{0.12 + 0.17}$$

This gives us a product of 0.41, or 41 percent.

Tunnel 7

The average offers are:

Situation 1
(eliminating a 1 in 1,000 risk): $800

Situation 2
(reducing risk from 4 in 1,000 to 3 in 1,000): $250

Situation 3
(voluntarily accepting a risk of 1 in 1,000): $100,000

The Birthday Problem

The correct answer is 24. With 36 people in the room, the probability rises to more than 90 percent. No one gives anything like these estimates intuitively; we all go much higher. (A classic answer is 183, which is arrived at by dividing the number of days in a year by two and then adding one, to have a better than 50 percent probability.)

Tunnel 8

The Hawaii Vacation

The results obtained by Shafir and Tversky at Stanford were:

Knowing the Result	Pass	Fail
Buy	54%	57%
Do not buy	16%	12%
Pay to wait for result	30%	31%
Not Knowing the Result		
Buy	32%	
Do not buy	7%	
Pay to wait for result	61%	

Comment: The percentage of students buying their vacation in a *certainty* situation, in which they know the result *either* way, is 55.5 percent. In an *uncertainty* situation, which logically should produce a comparable result, only 32 percent buy. The percentage of those paying to await certainty roughly doubles.

Second Round of Betting

Knowing They Have:	Won	Lost
Bet again	69%	59%
Don't bet again	31%	41%
Not Knowing		
Bet again	36%	
Don't bet again	64%	

Comment: Once again, the percentage of players accepting a second bet in a *certainty* situation (that is, knowing whether they've won or lost) is 64 percent. In *uncertainty* this falls to 36 percent. Symmetrically, the percentage of those who do not bet again, in *uncertainty*, rises to 64 percent (the theoretical average would be 36 percent). The highest "triplet" for a *single* subject, among the eight possible "triplets," is (implicitly, but demonstrably) as follows:

I bet again if I know I've won.

I bet again if I know I've lost.

I don't bet again if I don't know.

This "triplet" turns up in 65 percent of all respondents who said they would bet again if they knew they'd won or lost—in short, if they were certain of the result. For obvious reasons, this is the most interesting result in terms of the disjunction effect.

The *general* percentage of responses from the *same* respondents (answers that show the disjunction effect at its most clear and unequivocal form) is 65 percent. This figure is further confirmed by experiments in simulated competition (e.g., the prisoner's dilemma).

Main Sources

Arkes, H. R., and K. R. Hammond (eds.). *Judgement and Decision Making: An Interdisciplinary Reader.* Cambridge and New York: Cambridge University Press, 1986.

Bell, D. E., H. Raiffa, and A. Tversky (eds.). *Decision Making: Descriptive, Normative and Prescriptive Interactions.* Cambridge and New York: Cambridge University Press, 1988.

Elster, J. (ed.). *Rational Choice.* New York: New York University Press, 1986.

Gärdenfors, P., and N.-E. Sahlin (eds.). *Decision, Probability, and Utility: Selected Readings.* Cambridge and New York: Cambridge University Press, 1988.

Kahneman, D., P. Slovic, and A. Tversky (eds.). *Judgment under Uncertainty: Heuristics and Biases.* Cambridge and New York: Cambridge University Press, 1982.

Moser, P. K. (ed.). *Rationality in Action: Contemporary Approaches.* Cambridge and New York: Cambridge University Press, 1990.

Other General Sources

Bacharach, M., and S. Hurley (eds.). *Foundations of Decision Theory: Issues and Advances.* Oxford: Basil Blackwell, 1991.

Earman, J. *Bayes or Bust? A Critical Examination of Bayesian Confirmation Theory.* Cambridge, Mass.: Bradford Books/The MIT Press, 1992.

Evans, J. St. B. T. (ed.). *Thinking and Reasoning: Psychological Approaches.* London: Routledge & Kegan Paul, 1983.

Gigerenzer, G., and D. J. Murray. *Cognition as Intuitive Statistics.* Hillsdale, NJ: Lawrence Erlbaum, 1987.

Heap, S. H., M. Hollis, B. Lyons, R. Sugden, and A. Weale. *The Theory of Choice: A Critical Guide.* Oxford: Basil Blackwell, 1992.

Kreps, D. M. *Notes on the Theory of Choice,* London: Westview Press, 1988.

Johnson-Laird, P. N. *Mental Models: Towards a Cognitive Science of Language, Inference and Consciousness.* Cambridge, Mass.: Harvard University Press, 1983

Johnson-Laird, P. N., and E. Shafir (eds.). *Reasoning and Decision Making.* Special issue of *Cognition,* 49 (October–November 1993).

Johnson-Laird, P. N., and P. C. Wason (eds.). *Thinking: Readings in Cognitive Science.* Cambridge: Cambridge University Press, 1977.

Manktelow, K. I., and D. E. Over (eds.). *Rationality.* London: Routledge, 1993.

Nisbett, R. E., and L. Ross. *Human Inference: Strategies and Shortcomings of Social Judgement.* Englewood Cliffs, NJ: Prentice Hall, 1980.

Osherson, D. N., and E. E. Smith (eds.). *Thinking,* Vol. 3 of *An Invitation to Cognitive Science.* Cambridge, Mass.: MIT Press, 1990. (A revised and enlarged edition is forthcoming in 1994.)

Resnik, M. D. *Choices: An Introduction to Decision Theory.* Minneapolis: University of Minnesota Press, 1987.

Scholz, R. W. (ed.). *Decision Making under Uncertainty: Cognitive Decision Research, Social Interaction, Development and Epistemology.* Amsterdam and New York: Elsevier Science Publishers/North Holland, 1983.

Skyrms, B. *Choice and Chance: An Introduction to Inductive Logic.* Belmont, Calif.: Wadsworth, 1986.

Yates, J. F. *Judgment and Decision Making.* Englewood Cliffs, NJ: Prentice Hall, 1990.

Suggested Reading

The following offer the reader further insight into topics discussed within the text. However, it is fair to warn the reader that the majority of sources are written at a technical level that is higher than the one adopted in this book. Note, too, that the order in which the sources are listed follows the order in which the topics are presented in the book.

The use of the Gateway Arch in St. Louis as a vivid metaphor for cognitive illusions is due to Professor Richard H. Thaler of Cornell University:

Thaler, R. H., "Illusions and Mirages in Public Policy," *The Public Interest* 73: 60–74 (1983).

Also covered in Arkes and Hammond, *Judgement and Decision Making,* Chapter 9.

For the three-card problem and the experimental data on the Dutch bookability of real subjects:

Bar-Hillel, M. and R. Falk. "Some Teasers Concerning Conditional Probabilities," *Cognition* 11 (1982): 109–122.

Osherson, D. N. "Probability Judgment," in Osherson, D. N., E. E. Smith (eds.), *Thinking*, 2nd ed., Vol. 3 of *An Invitation to Cognitive Science* (Cambridge, Mass.: MIT Press, forthcoming, 1995.)

The Dutch bookie:
Jeffrey, R. C. *The Logic of Decision*, 2nd ed. (New York: McGraw-Hill, 1983.)

Jeffrey, R. C. "Probable Knowledge," in Gärdenfors and Sahlin, *Decision Probability and Utility*, pp. 86–96.

van Fraassen, B. C., "Belief and the Will," *The Journal of Philosophy* 81 (5) 235–256 (1984).

On the "Wittgenstein paradox":
Putnam, H. *Reason, Truth and History* (Cambridge, UK: Cambridge University Press, 1981).

Wittgenstein, L. *On Certainty* (Oxford: Basil Blackwell, 1969).

The beautiful sentence "neither rational nor capricious" is in:
Tversky, A., and D. Kahneman. "Advances in Prospect Theory: Cumulative Representation of Uncertainty," *Journal of Risk and Uncertainty*, 5 297–323 (1992).

On the intuitions about golgi and biotine see:
Osherson, D., E. Smith, O. Wilkie, A. Lopez, and E. Shafir. "Category-based Induction," *Psychological Review* 97: 185–200 (1990).

Mr. Baker's ticket and Mr. Jones's flight:
Kahneman, D., and A. Tversky. "The Simulation Heuristic," in Kahneman, Slovic, and Tversky, *Judgment under Uncertainty*.

Kahneman, D., and A. Tversky. "Choices, Values and Frames," *American Psychologist* 39 (4): 341–350.

Also covered in Arkes and Hammond, *Judgement and Decision Making*, Chapter 11.

For a survey of the notion of psychological "normality," and the strong affective reactions elicited by causes of events perceived as "abnormal":
Kahneman, D., and D. T. Miller. "Norm Theory: Comparing Reality to Its Alternatives," *Psychological Review* 93 (2): 136–153 (1986).

On the theory of "sunk cost" and its practical consequences:

Arkes, H. R., and C. Blumer. "The Psychology of Sunk Cost," *Organizational Behavior and Human Decision Processes* 35 (1): 124–130 (1985).

Thaler, R. H. *Quasi-Rational Economics*. (New York: Russell Sage Foundation Books, 1991).

On the theory of regret:

Bell, D. E. "Regret in Decision Making under Uncertainty," *Operations Research* 30: 361–381 (1982).

Fishburn, P. C. "Nontransitive Measurable Utility," *Journal of Mathematical Psychology* 26: 31–67 (1982).

Loomes, G., and R. Sugden. "Regret Theory: An Alternative Theory of Rational Choice under Uncertainty," *Economic Journal* 92: 805–824 (1982).

Loomes, G., and R. Sugden. "Some Implications of a More General Form of Regret Theory," *Journal of Economic Theory* 41: 270–287 (1987).

Machina, M. J. "Choice under Uncertainty: Problems Solved and Unsolved," *Economic Perspectives* 1 (1): 121–154 (1987).

For a recent review of the relations between expected utility, regret, and self-esteem:

Larrick, R. P. "Motivational Factors in Decision Theories: The Role of Self-Protection," *Psychological Bulletin* 113 (3): 440–450 (1993).

For a concise survey of the effects of cognitive illusions on managerial decision making:

Bazerman, M. H. *Judgment in Managerial Decision Making* (New York: John Wiley & Sons, 1990).

For a daily practice companion to decision making:

Russo, J. E., and P. J. H. Schoemaker. *Decision Traps: Ten Barriers to Brilliant Decision-making and How to Overcome Them* (New York: Doubleday, 1989).

For a presentation that manages to be both rigorous and entertaining:

Thaler, R. H. *The Winner's Curse: Paradoxes and Anomalies of Economic Life.* (New York: Russell Sage Foundation/Free Press, 1992).

For a more analytical, yet still quite engaging, survey of the effect of the main cognitive illusions on economics:

Thaler, R. H. *Quasi-Rational Economics* (New York: Russell Sage Foundation, 1991).

On the modularity of mind:

Fodor, Jerry A. *Modularity of Mind. An Essay in Faculty Psychology* (Cambridge, Mass.: MIT Press, 1983).

On Gregory's masks:

Gregory, R. L. *The Intelligent Eye* (London: Weidenfeld & Nicholson, 1970).

The thieves and composers syllogism:

Johnson-Laird, P. N. *Mental Models: Towards a Cognitive Science of Language, Inference and Consciousness* (Cambridge, Mass.: Harvard University Press, 1983).

The spirited exchange between Johnson-Laird and George Boolos is in:

Cognition 17: 181–182, 183–184 (1984).

For an updated review of syllogistic reasoning:

Evans, J. St. B. T., D. E. Over, and K. I. Manktelow. "Reasoning, Decision Making and Rationality," *Cognition* 49 (1–2): 165–187 (1993).

On the fast multiplication:

Tversky, A., and D. Kahneman. "Judgment under Uncertainty: Heuristics and Biases," *Science* 185: 1124–1131 (1974).

Also covered in Kahneman, Slovic, and Tversky, *Judgment under Uncertainty,* Chapter 1.

On the "imagined" frequency of words containing specific letters in specific positions:

Tversky, A., and D. Kahneman. "Availability: A Heuristic for Judging Frequency and Probability," *Cognitive Psychology* 4: 207–232 (1973).

Also covered in Kahneman, Slovic, and Tversky, *Judgment under Uncertainty,* Chapter 11.

On the statistical "balance" illusion in a short sequence of coins or dice tossing:

Kahneman, D., and A. Tversky. "Choices, Values and Frames," in Arkes and Hammond, *Judgement and Decision Making*.

Tversky, A., and D. Kahneman. "Belief in the Law of Small Numbers," in Kahneman, Slovic, and Tversky, *Judgment under Uncertainty*.

The framing of choices, the Asian disease, and realistic medical problems:

McNeil, B. J., S. G. Pauker, and A. Tversky, A. "On the Framing of Medical Decisions," in Bell, Raiffa, and Tversky, *Decision Making*.

McNeil, B. J., R. Weichselbaum, and S. G. Pauker. "Fallacy of the Five-Year Survival in Lung Cancer," *New England Journal of Medicine* 299: 1397–1401 (1978).

McNeil, B. J., S. G. Pauker, H. C. Sox Jr., and A. Tversky. "On the Elicitation of Preferences for Alternative Therapies," *New England Journal of Medicine* 306: 1259–1262 (1982).

Tversky, A., and D. Kahneman. "The Framing of Decisions and the Psychology of Choice," *Science* 211: 453–458 (1981).

Tversky, A., and D. Kahneman. "Rational Choice and the Framing of Decisions," in Bell, Raiffa, and Tversky, *Decision Making*, pp. 167–192.

Also covered in Arkes and Hammond, *Judgement and Decision Making*, Chapter 23.

Also covered in Elster, *Rational Choice*, Chapter 5.

On framing and segregation:

Bell, D. E., and H. Raiffa. "Risky Choice Revisited," in Bell, Raiffa, and Tversky, *Decision Making*.

Frisch, D. "Reasons for Framing Effects," *Organizational Behavior and Human Decision Processes* 54: 399–429 (1993).

Tversky, A., and D. Kahneman. "Advances in Prospect Theory: Cumulative Representation of Uncertainty," *Journal of Risk and Uncertainty* 5: 297–323 (1992).

Tversky, A., and D. Kahneman. "Rational Choice and the Framing of Decisions," in Bell, Raiffa, and Tversky, *Decision Making.*

On the theory of expected utility and its maximization as a "protection" from Dutch bookies:

Friedman, M., and L. J. Savage. "The Expected-Utility Hypothesis and the Measurability of Utility," *The Journal of Political Economy* 50 (6): 463–474 (1952).

Friedman, M., and L. J. Savage. "The Utility Analysis of Choices Involving Risk," *The Journal of Political Economy* 56 (4): 279–304 (1948).

Marschak, J. "Rational Behavior, Uncertain Prospects, and Measurable Utility," *Econometrica* 18: 111–141 (1950).

von Neumann, J., and O. Morgenstern. *Theory of Games and Economic Behavior* (Princeton, NJ: Princeton University Press, 1944; reprint 1990).

See also Resnik, Michael D., *Choices: An Introduction to Decision Theory* (Minneapolis, MN: University of Minnesota Press, 1987) and Gärdenfors, P., and N.-E. Sahlin, in Gärdenfors and Sahlin, *Decision, Probability, and Utility.*

For the "protection" offered by the Bayesian theory, see also below, under "Bayesian Theory."

On prospect theory:

Kahneman, D., and A. Tversky. "Prospect Theory: An Analysis of Decision under Risk," *Econometrica* 47: 263–291 (1979).

Tversky, A., and D. Kahneman. "Advances in Prospect Theory: Cumulative Representation of Uncertainty," *Journal of Risk and Uncertainty* 5: 297–323 (1992).

For the respective merits of the "advantage" and "prospect" models:

Shafir, E., D. N. Osherson, and E. E. Smith. "An Advantage Model of Choice," *Journal of Behavioral Decision Making* 2 (1): 1–23 (1989).

Shafir, E., D. N. Osherson, and E. E. Smith. "The Advantage Model: A Comparative Theory of Evaluation and Choice under Risk," *Organizational Behavior and Human Decision Processes* 55: 325–378 (1993).

Shafir, E., D. N. Osherson, and E. E. Smith. "Comparative Choice and the Advantage Model," in K. Borcherding, O. J. Larichev, and D. M. Messick (eds.), *Contemporary Issues in Decision Making* (Amsterdam and New York: Elsevier-North Holland, 1990).

On the conjunction effect:

Kahneman, D., and A. Tversky. "On the Psychology of Prediction," *Psychological Review* 80: 237–251 (1973).

Shafir, E., E. E. Smith, and D. N. Osherson. "Typicality and Reasoning Fallacies," *Memory and Cognition* 18 (3): 229–239 (1990).

Tversky, A., and D. Kahneman. "Extensional versus Intuitive Reasoning: The Conjunction Fallacy in Probability Judgment," *Psychological Review* 90 (4): 293–315 (1983).

Tversky, A., and D. Kahneman, "Judgment of and by Representativeness," in Kahneman, Slovic, and Tversky, *Judgment under Uncertainty.*

Also covered in Kahneman, Slovic, and Tversky, *Judgment under Uncertainty,* Chapter 4.

For a critique that claims to explain away the conjunction fallacy as a mere "linguistic" misunderstanding:

Fiedler, K. "The Dependence of the Conjunction Fallacy on Subtle Linguistic Factors," *Psychological Research* 50: 123–129 (1988).

For a critique based on collective frequencies, and not on intuitions on single cases (as in Bill and Linda) (see also Appendix B):

Gigerenzer, G. "How to Make Cognitive Illusions Disappear: Beyond 'Heuristics and Biases,'" *European Review of Social Psychology* 2: 83–115 (1991).

Gigerenzer, G., U. Hoffrage, and H. Kleinbölting. "Probabilistic Mental Models: A Brunswikian Theory of Confidence," *Psychological Review* 98 (4): 506–528 (1991).

Gigerenzer, G., and D. J. Murray. *Cognition as Intuitive Statistics* (Hillsdale, NJ: Lawrence Erlbaum, 1987).

For critiques of Tversky and Kahneman's entire research program, see Jonathan Cohen's article, and the ensuing "peer commentary":

Cohen, L. J. "Can Human Irrationality Be Experimentally Demonstrated?," *The Behavioral and Brain Sciences* 4: 317–331 (1981).

Smedslund, J. "A Critique of Tversky and Kahneman's Distinction between Fallacy and Misunderstanding," *Scandinavian Journal of Psychology* 31: 110–120 (1990).

For a uniquely well-balanced analysis of the merits and demerits of the "subjectivist" versus the "frequentistic" interpretation of probability, with special relevance to the problems presented here:

Kreps, D. M. *Notes on the Theory of Choice* (Boulder, Colo. and London: Westview Press, 1988).

On the base-rate fallacy:

Bar-Hillel, M. "The Base-rate Fallacy in Probability Judgments," *Acta Psychologica* 44: 211–233 (1980).

Einhorn, H. J., and R. M. Hogarth. "Behavioral Decision Theory: Processes of Judgment and Choice," *Annual Review of Psychology* 32: 53–88 (1981).

Nisbett, R. E., and E. Borgida. "Attribution and the Psychology of Prediction," *Journal of Personality and Social Psychology* 32 (5): 932–943 (1975).

Nisbett, R. E., and L. Ross. *Human Inference: Strategies and Shortcomings of Social Judgment* (Englewood Cliffs, NJ: Prentice Hall, 1980).

Tversky, A., and D. Kahneman. "Evidential Impact of Base Rates," in Kahneman, Slovic, and Tversky, *Judgment under Uncertainty.*

Also covered in Bell, Raiffa, and Tversky, *Decision Making,* Chapter 4.

On the social impact of typicality and of the neglect of base rates:

Taylor, S.E. "The Availability Bias in Social Perception and Interaction," in Kahneman, Slovic, and Tversky, *Judgment under Uncertainty.*

On hospitals, births, and the "maternity ward" problem:

Bar-Hillel, M. "The Role of Sample Size in Sample Evaluation," *Organizational Behavior and Human Performance* 24: 245–257 (1979).

Bar-Hillel, M. "Studies in Representativeness, 1982," in Kahnemann, Slovic, and Tversky, *Judgment under Uncertainty.*

Kahneman, D., and A. Tversky. "Subjective Probability: A Judgment of Representativeness," in Kahnemann, Slovic, and Tversky, *Judgment under Uncertainty.*

On the asymmetrical correlation between mother and daughter:

Tversky, A., and D. Kahneman. "Causal Schemas in Judgments under Uncertainty," in Fishbein (ed.), *Progress in Social Psychology* (Hillsdale, NJ: Lawrence Erlbaum, 1980).

Also covered in Kahnemann, Slovic, and Tversky, *Judgment under Uncertainty,* Chapter 8.

For a review of our spontaneous inclination to phrase simple reports of events in terms of causes and effects:

Weiner, B. "'Spontaneous' Causal Thinking," *Psychological Bulletin* 97 (1): 74–84 (1985).

The "clinical test":

Casscells, W., A. Schoenberger, and T. Grayboys. "Interpretation by Physicians of Clinical Laboratory Results," *New England Journal of Medicine* 299: 999–1000 (1978).

Eddy, D. M. "Probabilistic Reasoning in Clinical Medicine: Problems and Opportunities," in Kahneman, Slovic, and Tversky, *Judgment under Uncertainty.*

See also the paper, in press for *Cognition*, by Leda Cosmides and John Tooby, "Are Humans Good Intuitive Statisticians after All? Rethinking Some Conclusions from the Literature on Judgment under Uncertainty."

The "juror's fallacy" (or cab's problem):

Bar-Hillel, M. "The Base-Rate Fallacy in Probability Judgments," *Acta Psychologica* 44: 211–233 (1980).

Tversky, A., and D. Kahneman. "Evidential Impact of Base Rates," in Kahneman, Slovic, and Tversky, *Judgment under Uncertainty.*

A classic primer in the discovery of the neglect of base rates is:

Meehl, P., and A. Rosen. "Antecedent Probability and the Efficiency of Psychometric Signs, Patterns, or Cutting Scores," *Psychological Bulletin* 52: 194–215 (1955).

On cognitive illusions and judicial proceedings:

Saks, M. J., and R. F. Kidd. "Human Information Processing and Adjudication: Trial by Heuristics," *Law and Society Review* 15 (1): 123–160 (1980).

Also covered in Arkes and Hammond, *Judgement and Decision Making*, Chapter 12.

Hume's justly celebrated skeptical arguments about miracles:
Hume, D., *An Inquiry Concerning Human Understanding*, section 10 (Westport, CT: Greenwood Press, 1980).

See also, on Hume and the Bayesian calculation:
Owen, D. "Hume versus Price on Miracles and Prior Probabilities: Testimony and the Bayesian Calculation," *The Philosophical Quarterly* 147 (37): 187–202 and bibliography (1987).

The quite illuminating "strange virus" test is due to Richard H. Thaler:
Thaler, R. H. "Illusions and Mirages in Public Policy," *The Public Interest* 73: 60–74 (1983).

Also covered in Arkes and Hammond, *Judgement and Decision Making*, Chapter 9.

The certainty effect was introduced for the first time in:
Tversky, A., and D. Kahneman. "The Framing of Decisions and the Psychology of Choice," *Science* 211: 453–458 (1981).

Also covered in Elster, *Rational Choice*, Chapter 5.

On the misinterpretation of risk and the "special" insurance policy:
Hogarth, R. M. (ed.). *New Directions for Methodology of Social and Behavioral Science: The Framing of Questions and the Consistency of Responses* (San Francisco: Jossey-Bass, 1982).

Schwing, R., and W. A. Albers, (eds.). *Societal Risk Assessment: How Safe Is Safe Enough?* (New York: Plenum Press, 1980).

Slovic, P., B. Fischhoff, and S. Lichtenstein. "Facts versus Fears: Understanding Perceived Risk," in Schwing and Albers, *Societal Risk Assessment*.

Slovic, P., B. Fischhoff, and S. Lichtenstein. "Response Mode, Framing, and Information Processing," in Hogarth, *New Directions*, pp. 21–36.

Also covered in Bell, Raiffa, and Tversky, *Decision Making*, Chapter 8.

Also covered in Kahneman, Slovic, and Tversky, *Judgment Under Uncertainty*, Chapter 33.

On the uncertainty effect, or irrational prudence:

Shafir, E. B., and A. Tversky. "Thinking Through Uncertainty: Non-consequential Reasoning and Choice," *Cognitive Psychology* (in press).

Tversky, A., and E. Shafir. "The Disjunction Effect in Choice under Uncertainty," *Psychological Science* 3 (5): 305–309 (1992).

On the prisoner's dilemma, see Resnik, *Choices* and several contributions collected in Moser, *Rationality in Action,* and in Elster, *Rational Choices.*

The "sure-thing" principle:

Savage, L. J. "The Sure-Thing Principle," in *The Foundations of Statistics,* pp. 21–26 (New York: John Wiley & Sons, 1954; reprint, New York: Dover, 1972).

Also covered in Gärdenfors and Sahlin, *Decision, Probability, and Utility,* pp. 80–86.

The anecdote on Bohr comes from:

Shafir and Tversky, "Thinking through Uncertainty," *Cognitive Psychology* (in press).

On the paradoxes of voter behavior:

Meehl, P. E. "The Selfish Voter Paradox and the Thrown-Away Vote Argument," *The American Political Science Review* 71: 11–30 (1977).

Shafir, E. "Prospect Theory and Political Analysis: A Psychological Perspective," *Political Psychology* 13 (2): 311–322 (1992).

Data on the physician's excessive caution and on the overabundance of clinical tests are reported and analyzed in:

Allman, R. M., E. P. Steinberg, J. C. Keruly, and P. E. Dans. "Physicians Tolerance for Uncertainty: Use of Liver-Spleen Scans to Detect Metastases," *Journal of the American Medical Association* 254: 246–248 (1985).

Baron, J., J. Beattie, and J. C. Hershey. "Heuristics and Biases in Diagnostic Reasoning: (II). Congruence, Information, and Certainty," *Organizational Behavior and Human Decision Processes* 42: 88–110 (1988).

Kassirer, J. P. "Our Stubborn Quest for Diagnostic Certainty," *New England Journal of Medicine* 320: 1489–1491 (1989).

On the Bayesian theory:

Bayes, T. "An Essay Towards Solving a Problem in the Doctrine of Chances," *Philosophical Transactions of the Royal Society* 53: 370–418 (1763).

Bayes, T. "An Essay Towards Solving a Problem in the Doctrine of Chances," (reprint of the 1763 article), *Biometrika* 45: 296–315 (1958).

Earman, J. *Bayes or Bust? A Critical Examination of Bayesian Confirmation Theory* (Cambridge, Mass.: Bradford Books/MIT Press, 1992).

Eddy, D. M. "Probabilistic Reasoning in Clinical Medicine: Problems and Opportunities," in Kahneman, Slovic, and Tversky, *Judgment under Uncertainty.*

Edwards, W. "Conservatism in Human Information Processing," in B. Kleinmuntz (ed.), *Formal Representation of Human Judgment* (New York: John Wiley & Sons, 1968).

Fischhoff, B., and R. Beyth-Marom. "Hypothesis Evaluation from a Bayesian Perspective," *Psychological Review* 90 (3): 239–260 (1983).

Osherson, D. N., M. Stob, and S. Weinstein. "Mechanical Learners Pay a Price for Bayesianism," *The Journal of Symbolic Logic* 53 (4): 1245–1251 (1988).

Osherson, D. N., E. E. Smith, and E. B. Shafir. "Some Origins of Belief," *Cognition* 24: 197–224 (1986).

Also covered in Kahneman, Slovic, and Tversky, *Judgment Under Uncertainty,* Chapter 25.

The third part of the collection edited by Bell, Raiffa, and Tversky, *Judgment under Uncertainty,* contains four fundamental papers, including the "classic" work on the semantics of probability languages by G. Shafer and A. Tversky, "Languages and Designs for Probability Judgment," first published in *Cognitive Science* 9: 309–339 (1985).

On overconfidence:

Fischhoff, B., P. Slovic, and S. Lichtenstein. "Knowing with Certainty: The Appropriateness of Extreme Confidence," *Journal of Experimental Psychology: Human Perception and Performance* 3: 552–564 (1977).

Fischhoff, B. "Debiasing," in Kahneman, Slovic, and Tversky, *Judgment under Uncertainty.*

And the "classics":

Lichtenstein, S., B. Fischhoff, and L. D. Phillips. "Calibration of Probabilities: The State of the Art to 1980," in Kahneman, Slovic, and Tverksy, *Judgment under Uncertainty.*

Oskamp, S. "Overconfidence in Case-Study Judgments," in Kahneman, Slovic, and Tversky, *Judgment under Uncertainty.*

For an attempt to deemphasize overconfidence (see also Appendix B):

Gigerenzer, G. "How to Make Cognitive Illusions Disappear: Beyond Heuristics and Biases," *European Review of Social Psychology* 2: 83–115 (1991).

On overconfidence as an effect of outcome knowledge:

Fischhoff, B. "Hindsight is Not Foresight: The Effect of Outcome Knowledge on Judgment under Uncertainty," *Journal of Experimental Psychology: Human Perception and Performance* 1: 288–299 (1975).

On the rise of overconfidence with greater expertise, and on the dangers of overconfidence in social prediction:

Dunning, D., D. W. Griffin, J. D. Milojkovic, and L. Ross. "The Overconfidence Effect in Social Prediction," *Journal of Personality and Social Psychology* 58 (4): 568–581 (1990).

Vallone, R. P., D. W. Griffin, S. Lin, and L. Ross. "Overconfident Prediction of Future Actions and Outcomes by Self and Others," *Journal of Personality and Social Psychology* 58 (4): 582–592 (1990).

Wagenar, W. A., and G. B. Keren. "Does the Expert Know? The Reliability of Predictions and Confidence Ratings of Experts," in E. Hollnagel, G. Maneini, D. Woods (eds.), *Intelligent Decision Support in Process Environments*, NATO-ASI Series, Vol. F21 (Berlin: Springer-Verlag, 1986).

On illusory correlations and magic thinking:

Chapman, L. J. "Illusory Correlation in Observational Report," *Journal of Verbal Learning and Verbal Behavior* 6: 151–155 (1967).

Chapman, L. J., and J. P. Chapman. "Illusory Correlation as an Obstacle to the Use of Valid Psychodiagnostic Signs," *Journal of Abnormal Psychology* 74(3): 271–280 (1969).

Chapman, L. J., and J. Chapman. "Test Results Are What You Think They Are," *Psychology Today,* pp. 18–22, 106–110 (November 1971).

Also covered in Kahneman, Slovic, and Tversky, *Judgment under Uncertainty,* Chapter 17.

On the bias of concentrating statistical correlation in only one of the four possible cases (disease present—test positive), see the recent data in:

Lewin, I. P., E. A. Waserman, and S.-F. Kao. "Multiple Methods for Examining Biased Information Use in Contingency Judgments," *Organizational Behavior and Human Decision Processes* 55: 228–250 (1993).

For a recent review, and new data, on the "hindsight bias" see:

Creyer, E., W. T. Ross, Jr. "Hindsight Bias and Inferences in Choice: The Mediating Effect of Cognitive Effort," *Organizational Behavior and Human Decision Processes* 55: 61–77 (1993).

On the "selection task" and on our natural inclination toward "confirmation" rather than "refutation":

Edwards, W., "Conservatism in Human Information Processing," in B. Kleinmuntz (ed.), *Formal Representation of Human Judgment* (New York: John Wiley & Sons, 1968).

Wason, P. C. "On the Failure to Eliminate Hypotheses in a Conceptual Task," *Quarterly Journal of Experimental Psychology* 12: 129–140 (1960).

Wason, P. C. "Realism and Rationality in the Selection Task," in St. J. B. Evans (ed.), *Thinking and Reasoning: Psychological Approaches* (London: Routledge & Kegan Paul, 1983).

Wason, P. C. "Reasoning," in B. M. Foss (eds.), *New Horizons in Psychology,* Vol. 1 (London: Penguin, 1966).

Wason, P. C. "Reasoning about a Rule," *Quarterly Journal of Experimental Psychology* 20: 273–281 (1968).

Also covered in Kahneman, Slovic, and Tversky, *Judgment under Uncertainty,* Chapter 25.

For evidence of improvement and facilitation in the selection task, when the situation looks natural and familiar to the subject, see:

Cheng, P. W., and K. J. Holyoak. "Pragmatic Reasoning Schemas," *Cognitive Psychology* 17: 391–416 (1985).

For the more recent "evolutionistic" approach to the problem (discussed in Appendix B):

Cosmides, L. "The Logic of Social Exchange: Has Natural Selection Shaped How Humans Reason? Studies with the Wason Selection Task," *Cognition* 33: 285–313 (1989).

Gigerenzer, G. and K. Hug. "Domain-Specific Reasoning: Social Contracts, Cheating, and Perspective Change," *Cognition* 43: 127–171 (1992).

For a critical discussion of this "evolutionistic" approach:

Cheng, P. W., and K. J. Holyoak. "On the Natural Selection of Reasoning Theories," *Cognition* 33: 285–313 (1989).

For an application of the selection task to clinical diagnosis:

Arkes, H. R. "Impediments to Accurate Clinical Judgment and Possible Ways to Minimize Their Impact," *Consulting and Clinical Psychology* 49 (3): 323–330 (1981).

Also covered in Arkes and Hammond, *Judgement and Decision Making,* Chapter 36.

For the "falsificationist" nature of science:

Popper, K. *The Logic of Scientific Discovery* (New York: Basic Books, 1949; originally Vienna, 1935).

On the "historian's fallacies":

Dray, R. "Historians' Fallacies," in Arkes and Hammond, *Judgement and Decision Making.*

Fischer, D. H. *Historians' Fallacies* (New York: Harper and Row, 1970).

Fischhoff, B. "For Those Condemned to Study the Past: Heuristics and Biases in Hindsight," in Kahneman, Slovic, and Tversky, *Judgment under Uncertainty,*

On anchoring and the wheel of fortune:

Quattrone, G. A. "Overattribution and Unit Formation: When Behavior Engulfs the Person," *Journal of Personality and Social Psychology* 42 (4): 593–607 (1982).

Tversky, A., and D. Kahneman. "Judgment under Uncertainty: Heuristics and Biases," *Science* 185: 1124–1131 (1974).

See also Kahneman, Slovic, and Tversky, *Judgment under Uncertainty*, Chapters 1, 33; and Bell, Raiffa, and Tversky, *Decision Making*, Chapters 8, 18.

The quotation from Bertrand Russell is in Bertrand Russull, *Philosophy* (New York: Norton, 1927).

On the birthday "coincidence":

Diaconis, P. "Statistical Problems in ESP Research," *Science* 201: 131–136 (1978).

The nineteenth-century conversation manual for German tourists containing a section on what to say in case of incarceration is:

Radicchi, G., and F. Bozzi. *Conversations Taschenbuch der Italienischer Sprache*, 5th ed. (Vienna: Lechner's Universitäts Buchhandlung, 1847).

On probability blindness:

Piattelli-Palmarini, M. "Probability Blindness: Neither Rational Nor Capricious," *Bostonia*, pp. 28–35 (March/April 1991).

On reconsideration under suitable scripts:

Einhorn, H. J., and R. M. Hogarth. "Confidence in Judgment: Persistence of the Illusion of Validity," *Psychological Review* 85: 395–416 (1978).

Wallsten, T. S. (ed.). *Cognitive Processes in Choice and Decision Behavior* (Hillsdale, NJ: Lawrence Erlbaum, 1980).

On the crisis of logic and the demise of "naive" set theory, the arch-classic is:

Kneale, W., and M. Kneale. *The Development of Logic* (Oxford: Oxford University Press, 1962; reprint, 1986)

On the principle of identity and the psychology of typicality:

Medin, D. L., R. L. Goldstone, and D. Gentner. "Respects for Similarity," *Psychological Review* 100 (2): 254–278 (1993).

Osherson, D., E. Smith, O. Wilkie, A. Lopez, and E. Shafir. "Category-based Induction," *Psychological Review* 97: 185–200 (1990).

Rosch, E. "Principles of Categorization," in E. Rosch, and B. B. Lloyd (eds.), *Cognition and Categorization*, pp. 27–48 (Hillsdale, NJ: Lawrence Erlbaum, 1978).

Smith, E. "Categorization," in D. N. Osherson, and E. E. Smith, (eds.), *An Invitation to Cognitive Science*, Vol. 3, *Thinking*, pp. 33–53 (Cambrdge, Mass.: MIT Press, 1990).

Smith, E., D. Osherson, L. Rips, and M. Keane. "Combining Prototypes: A Selective Modification Model," *Cognitive Science* 12: 485–527 (1988).

Tversky, A. "Features of Similarity," *Psychological Review* 84: 327–352 (1977).

Tversky, A. and I. Gati. "Studies of Similarity," in E. Rosch and B. Lloyd (eds.), *Cognition and Categorization*, pp. 79–98 (Hillsdale, NJ: Lawrence Erlbaum, 1978).

On the stronger "typicality" of certain even or odd numbers:

Armstrong, S. L., L. R. Gleitman, and H. Gleitman. "What Some Concepts Might Not Be," *Cognition* 13: 263–308 (1983).

On our curious mental representations of numbers, and on the psychology of simple arithmetic tasks:

Dehaene, S., and J. Mehler. "Cross-Linguistic Regularities in the Frequency of Number Words," *Cognition* 43: 1–30 (1992).

Deahene, S., S. Bossini, and P. Giraux. "The Mental Representation of Parity and Number Magnitude," *Journal of Experimental Psychology: General* 122 (3): 371–398 (1993).

Frensch, P. A., and D. C. Geary. "Effects of Practice on Component Processes in Complex Mental Addition," *Journal of Experimental Psychology: Learning, Memory and Cognition* 19 (2): 433–456 (1993).

McCloskey, M., A. Caramazza, and A. Basili. "Cognitive Mechanisms in Number Processing and Calculation: Evidence from Dyscalculia," *Brain and Cognition* 10: 46–60 (1985).

On the super-tunnel (the Monty Hall paradox and the three prisoners dilemma):
Falk, R. "A Closer Look at the Probabilities of the Notorious Three Prisoners," *Cognition* 43 (3): 197–223 (1992).

Gardner, M. *The Second Scientific American Book of Mathematical Puzzles and Diversions* (New York: Simon and Schuster, 1961).

Gillman, L. "The car and the goats," *The American Mathematical Monthly* 99 (1): 3–7 (January 1992).

Piattelli-Palmarini, M., "Probability Blindness."

For a history of the evolution of these studies, with particular attention to the effects on clinical decision:
Kleinmuntz, B. "The Scientific Study of Clinical Judgment in Psychology and Medicine," *Clinical Psychology Review* 4: 111–126 (1984).

Also covered in Arkes and Hammond, *Judgement and Decision Making*, Chapter 34.

For an overview of the effects on economic decision making:
Slovic, P. "Psychological Study of Human Judgment: Implications for Investment Decision Making," *Journal of Finance* 27 (4): 779–799 (1972).

Also covered in Arkes and Hammond, *Judgement and Decision Making*, Chapter 10.

Also covered in Thaler, *The Winner's Curse* and Thaler, *Quasi-Rational Economics*.

See also the first chapters of Kahneman, Slovic, and Tversky, *Judgment under Uncertainty;* Gärdenfors and Sahlin, *Decision, Probability, and Utility;* and Osherson and Smith, *Thinking: An Invitation to Cognitive Science*, vol. 3.

On the transition from Piagetism to modern cognitive science, see the debate between Noam Chomsky and Jean Piaget in:

Piattelli-Palmarini, M. "Ever Since Language and Learning: Afterthoughts on the Piaget-Chomsky Debate," *Cognition,* pp. 315–346 (1994).

Piattelli-Palmarini, M. (ed.). *Language and Learning: The Debate between Jean Piaget and Noam Chomsky* (Cambridge, Mass.: Harvard University Press, 1980).

The following list is a concise selection (in alphabetical order) of some historical milestones and recent "classics" in the field at large:

Allais, M. "Le comportement de l'homme rationnel devant le risque: Critique des postulats et axiomes de l'école américaine," *Econometrica* 21: 503–546 (1953). English translation: Chap. 5 of Moser, *Rationality in Action.*

Bruner, J. S., J. J. Goodnow, and G. A. Austin. *A Study of Thinking* (New York: John Wiley & Sons, 1956).

Edwards, W. "The Theory of Decision Making," *Psychological Bulletin* 51: 380–417 (1954).

Ellsberg, D. "Risk, Ambiguity, and the Savage Axioms," *Quarterly Journal of Economics* 75: 643–669 (1961).

Friedman, M., and L. J. Savage. "The Expected-Utility Hypothesis and the Measurability of Utility," *Journal of Political Economy* 60: 463–474 (1952).

Friedman, M. and L. J. Savage. "The Utility Analysis of Choices Involving Risk," *Journal of Political Economy* 56: 279–304 (1948).

Goodman, N. *Fact, Fiction and Forecast* (Cambridge, Mass.: Harvard University Press, 1983; reprint of the 1954 original).

Holt, R. R. "Yet Another Look at Clinical and Statistical Prediction," *American Psychologist* 25: 337–339 (1970).

Knight, F. H. *Risk, Uncertainty, and Profit* (Boston: Houghton-Mifflin, 1921).

Luce, R. D. and Raiffa, H. "Individual Decision Making under Uncertainty," in *Games and Decisions*, pp. 275–306 (New York: John Wiley & Sons, 1957).

Lusted, L. B. *Introduction to Medical Decision Making* (Springfield, Ill.: C. C. Thomas, 1968).

Marschak, J. "Rational Behavior, Uncertain Prospects, and Measurable Utility," *Econometrica* 18: 111–114 (1950).

Meehl, P. E. *Clinical Versus Statistical Prediction: A Theoretical Analysis and a Review of the Evidence* (Minneapolis: University of Minnesota Press, 1954).

Peterson, C. R., and L. R. Beach. "Man as an Intuitive Statistician," *Psychological Bulletin* 68: 29–46 (1967).

Savage, L. J. *The Foundations of Statistics* (New York: John Wiley & Sons, 1954).

Sells, S. B. "The Atmosphere Effect: An Experimental Study of Reasoning," *Archivia Psychologica* 29: 3–72 (1936).

Simon, H. A. "Rational Choice and the Structure of the Environment," *Psychological Review* 63: 129–138 (1956).

Slovic, P. B. Fischhoff, and S. Lichtenstein. "Behavioral Decision Theory," *Annual Reviews of Psychology* 28: 1–39 (1977).

See also Savage, L. J. "Allais' Paradox," in Gärdenfors and Sahlin, *Decision, Probability, and Utility*.

For a new approach to the normative theory:

Kelly, K. T., and C. Glymour. "Convergence to the Truth and Nothing but the Truth," *Philosophy of Science* 56: 183–220 (1989).

Osherson, D. N., M. Stob, and S. Weinstein. "Mechanical Learners Pay a Price for Bayesianism," *The Journal of Symbolic Logic* 53 (4): 1245–1250 (1988).

Osherson, D., M. Stob, and S. Weinstein. *Systems That Learn* (Cambridge, Mass.: MIT Press, 1986).

Osherson, D., M. Stob, S. Weinstein. "Paradigms of Truth Detection," *Journal of Philosophical Logic* 18: 1–42 (1989).

For an all-round collective attempt to root cognition into Darwinian adaptation to the environment, see:

Barkow, J. H., L. Cosmides, and J. Tooby. *The Adapted Mind: Evolutionary Psychology and the Generation of Culture* (Oxford and New York: Oxford University Press, 1992).

Selected references of works by G. Gigerenzer, et al.:

Gigerenzer, G. "The Bounded Rationality of Probabilistic Mental Models," in K. I. Manktelow and D. E. Over (eds.), *Rationality* (London, Routledge & Kegan Paul, 1993).

Gigerenzer, G. "From Tools to Theories: A Heuristic of Discovery in Cognitive Psychology," *Psychological Review* 98 (2): 254–267 (1991).

Gigerenzer, G. "How to Make Cognitive Illusions Disappear: Beyond 'Heuristics and Biases,'" *European Review of Social Psychology* 2: 83–115 (1991).

Gigerenzer, G., and K. Hug. "Domain-Specific Reasoning: Social Contracts, Cheating, and Perspective Change," *Cognition* 4: 127–171 (1992).

Gigerenzer, G., W. Hell, and H. Blank. "Presentation and Content: The Use of Base Rates as a Continuous Variable," *Journal of Experimental Psychology, General* 14 (3): 513–525 (1988).

Gigerenzer, G., U. Hoffrage, and H. Kleinbölting. "Probabilistic Mental Models: A Brunswikian Theory of Confidence," *Psychological Review* 98 (4): 506–528 (1991).

Gigerenzer, G., Z. Switjink, T. Porter, L. J. Daston, J. Beatty, and L. Krüger. *The Empire of Chance: How Probability Changed Science and Everyday Life.* (Cambridge, UK: Cambridge University Press, 1989).

Kruger, L., G. Gigerenzer, and M. S. Morgan, (ed.). *The Probabilistic Revolution* (Cambridge, Mass.: MIT Press, 1987).

A remarkable instance of the impact of emotionally charged single cases on decision making is the indelible impression made on Ronald Reagan by the predicament of his "overtaxed" friend, with momentous consequences on Reagan's fiscal policy as a whole:

Stockman, D. A. *The Triumph of Politics: Why the Reagan Revolution Failed* (New York: Harper and Row, 1986).

The "particularly nasty" critical article is:

Lopes, L. L. "The Rhetoric of Irrationality," *Theory and Psychology* 1: 65–82 (1991).

The stunning story of insect mouthpieces having evolved long before there were any flowers on Earth is told in:

Labandeira, C. C., and J. J. Sepkoski. "Insect Diversity in the Fossil Record," *Science* 261: 310–314 (1993).

For a recent review of the success of a non-adaptationist theory of evolution:

Gould, S. J., and N. Eldredge. "Punctuated Equilibrium Comes of Age," *Nature* 366: 223–227 (1993).

Index